STEAM AND SPEED

The townscape and transport focus of Newcastle was fundamentally changed by the coming of the railway. Thomas Hair's watercolour of c.1850 captures the view down St Nicholas' Street, the new approach to the High Level Bridge, as the railway viaduct cuts between the Norman Castle and the Black Gate.

STEAM AND SPEED

Railways of Tyne and Wear
from the Earliest Days

Andy Guy

Tyne Bridge Publishing
Newcastle Libraries & Information Service

Acknowledgements:

Newcastle Libraries would like to thank the J.W. Armstrong Trust; Beamish North of England Open Air Museum, particularly Jim Lawson; Bowes Railway; Sheila Bye; Agnes Chilton; the Ken Hoole Study Centre, Darlington Railway Centre and Museum; Deutsches Museum, Munich; Trevor Ermel; Gateshead Libraries & Arts; Helen Gomersall; Ironbridge Gorge Museum Trust; Tony Liddell; the McDowell Trust Collection-Stephenson Locomotive Society (Newcastle Centre); Alan Morgan; National Railways Museum, York; the Highways and Planning Section at Newcastle City Council, particularly Ian Ayris; North Tyneside Libraries; North East Locomotive Preservation Group; Northumberland Record Office; N.E. Stead; Tanfield Railway; Tyne & Wear Archives; Tyne & Wear Museums.

Illustrations Acknowledgements: Copyright and provenance of illustrations is indicated wherever possible. Other illustrations are reproduced courtesy of Newcastle Libraries. The maps on pages 139 and 153 were drawn by Tony Liddell.

©Andy Guy, 2003

Published by City of Newcastle upon Tyne
Education & Libraries Directorate
Newcastle Libraries & Information Service
Tyne Bridge Publishing, 2003

ISBN 1857951611

Printed by Elanders Hindson, North Tyneside

Front cover:

Class 4A locomotive No. 60019 *Bittern* stands at Newcastle Central Station on the evening of 4 November 1967, with the return leg of a Leeds to Edinburgh enthusiasts' special train.

A Gateshead-based engine for much of its working life, *Bittern* had been withdrawn from service the previous year and was by this time privately-owned, one of six A4s to survive into preservation.
Photograph ©Trevor Ermel

Back cover:

The *Steam Elephant* at Wallsend, c.1820, the earliest surviving 'fine art' representation of a locomotive. A working replica runs at Beamish. Oil on canvas, courtesy of the North of England Open Air Museum, Beamish.

Find Tyne Bridge Publishing at tynebridgepublishing.co.uk for a full range of North East history titles.

Young North Eastern Railway cleaners grouped on a 'BTP' locomotive, Wearside, c.1900. Tyne & Wear Museums

Contents

Andy Guy – Tanfield Railway

Children outside a Newcastle sweet shop c.1890. Boys (and men) have been fascinated by trains since the earliest days – at the Newcastle Polytechnic exhibition of 1840, 'there was a model Railway of circular form where an engine and train kept running round'.

The Cradle of the Railways

If the North East has given one great gift to the world, it is the modern railway. And if there is one figure from the region renowned around the world it is George Stephenson. The origins of both lie within a few miles of Newcastle, and they have left a visual and a historical stamp upon the area. This is not a book about the beauty of big – or little – steam engines, nor does it attempt the definitive history of the region's railways. It takes an affectionate look at some of the features of Tyneside and Wearside that reflect the development of the railway and how its success changed the North East.

Rail today is to some extent marginalised, trapped between the long distance advantages of airtravel and the personal convenience of the road. However, in its day it was the first mechanical transport to be in general use, superseding the natural limits of animal transport for the first time. The railway's ability to move the industrial staples of coal and iron cheaply brought the Industrial Revolution to maturity. It reduced the advantages held by the areas of production, to stimulate growth elsewhere; it enabled the supply of fresh foods to feed the growing towns; it encouraged suburban housing; it even led to the development of the great seaside resorts. The railway changed perceptions of time and speed, it unified countries and continents. For more than a century it was the basis of overland freight and passenger travel. It was perhaps the greatest single factor in the creation of the modern industrial world.

The role of Tyne and Wear in the development of the railway is unique. During the eighteenth century the complex network of horse waggonways from the collieries to the colliers made a deep impression on visitors. As the wooden ways developed into the powered iron railway, it was on the Newcastle system that they were modelled and built. From the North East came John Blenkinsop, and Matthew Murray, who developed the first economic locomotives; William Hedley and Timothy Hackworth, builders of *Puffing Billy* and *Wylam Dilly*; Longridge and Birkinshaw who solved the problems of rails; and the greatest single influence of all, George Stephenson. The evidence of how, why, when and where these historic events took place are impressed upon the cities of Newcastle, Sunderland and the surrounding area, and can still remind us of the extraordinary effect the railway had on changing the everyday world.

*Stephenson's **Billy**, presented to Newcastle, graced the north end of the High Level Bridge then later the Central Station – a symbol of the area's role in railway history. NLIS*

This Trade of Coals

The story of the railways does not start with George Stephenson, Newcastle or even the North East. The first on record originated in Ancient Greece around 600 BC. One, the 'Diolkos', ran across the neck of land separating the Gulf of Corinth from the Saronic Gulf and, remarkably, was used to carry large boats from one seaway to the other. There is evidence that they were also used in mineral mines of the Roman Empire, so that when the railway is clearly seen again in similar mines in Germany in the fifteenth century, it may be that the knowledge of them had been retained rather than rediscovered.

It was some time before they appeared in Britain, and the impetus was the greatly increased production of coal. It has been estimated that Britain was mining some 210,000 tons a year in the 1550s but nearly three million by the 1680s, with the total from the North East rising from 65,000 tons to 1,225,000. The 'Great Northern Coalfield' of Durham and Northumberland shipped to markets on the east coast of England and dominated the supply to London. It was essential to transport coal from inland pits to the loading staiths on the Tyne and the Wear. Without the railway this heavy, bulky but surprisingly fragile load had to be moved either by cart (locally, a 'wain') or by packhorse, requiring huge numbers of horses, oxen, vehicles and men. Whickham colliery, just south of the Tyne, for example, was using some 700 wains a day by the end of the sixteenth century and it can be imagined what this further implied in terms of stabling, feed, harness and repairs.

The public roads were often little more than unmade tracks, dusty in the summer, churned into thick mud in the rain and often impassable in the winter snows. They were ill-fitted to take on the massive additional traffic of the collieries, whilst the slowness of the carts added to both the cost and unpredictability of coal production. Transport became a bottleneck to the expansion of the coal trade. A common alternative was to construct a dedicated 'wainway' direct from the pits to the staith, but again the weight of traffic caused problems to the road surface and often all transport of the coals had to be abandoned for much of the winter. A more efficient and consistent system was desperately needed.

An engraving of a German mine railway, from Agricola's De Re Metallica, *1556.*

The first definite evidence for a railway, or waggonway as it was more commonly called, emerges around 1603 at Wollaton pits in Nottinghamshire. It seems to have been a great success, expanding production and avoiding a local cartway which was described as 'so foul as few carriages can pass'. It was worked by Huntingdon Beaumont, who also had coal interests in Northumberland. He built three waggonways from his pits at Bedlington, Bebside and Cowpen down to the River Blyth, perhaps as early as 1605, and so the railway came to the North East in the earliest days of its existence in England.

Little good it did to Mr Beaumont, however. He arrived in the area with a large fortune and a host of new mining techniques, but left less than ten years later having 'consumed all his money and rode home upon his light horse', dying, deeply in debt, in 1624. But his waggonway system was slowly taken up. By 1649 Gray could write in his survey of Newcastle, *Chorographia*, 'Many thousand people are employed in this trade of coals; many live by conveying them in wagons and waines to the river Tyne'. Little is known about these early routes but it seems likely that the first to serve the Tyne was at Whickham, where the pits had needed such a vast number of wains.

The growth in coal production faltered with the coming of the Civil War and Cromwell's Commonwealth. Many of the great northern owners had backed the losing side and had their estates confiscated or were heavily fined, royalty leases were disputed and there were some dubious transactions by the victors over their spoils. The Restoration returned a degree of stability to the coal trade but it remained vulnerable to deep recessions throughout the late seventeenth and early eighteenth centuries.

However, average production continued to grow with a match-

Waggonway horses became so practised that they needed the minimum of 'driving'. The Dixon family of Cockfield were to have strong railway connections. One acted as assistant to George Stephenson on his early lines, another built the first railway in China. And yet another surveyed the 'Mason-Dixon' slavery boundary in America, hence 'Dixieland'

ing increase in the sophistication of its systems. This stimulated the development of a remarkable waggonway system in the region. As the older collieries near the Tyne became exhausted or flooded out, it became necessary to sink pits further and further from the river. This could only amplify the advantages of the waggonway over the wainway. Where common coal carts might carry less than a ton and require perhaps four horses or oxen, the railway waggon could hold twice as much and usually needed just one horse. Not only were the potential savings very great, but the waggonway was far more reliable than a roadway, with all its vulnerability to the weather. The further the pit was from the loading staith, the greater became the advantages of a railway.

This was not without a cost of course. A proper trackbed had to be built, firm and well drained, with the sleepers covered to

This vignette from John Gibson's coalfield map of 1787 shows an idealised colliery scene, the loaded waggon descending a graded line to the staith, horse following, driver sitting on the brake, then the gruelling return uphill.

make a good surface for the horses, to provide a consistent width or 'gauge' for the lines, and rails sawn and securely fastened. Ideally, there would be a gentle gradient down to the river to reduce the work needed by the horse, which could then pull the empty waggon back up. Most of all, it was important to reduce, as far as possible, the need to pull a full load uphill, but geography is seldom so helpful and it was often necessary to make cuttings, embankments and bridges. Not only was the construction relatively expensive but constant maintenance was needed so that both the initial and running costs were substantial.

As a result, the early waggonways were most effective for the larger collieries, although, as the eighteenth century progressed, some owners found that they could combine their routes and reduce their expense. Smaller pits, or those that sold their coal locally as 'landsale' rather than 'seasale' might not find these costs effective or necessary, but in general, by the 1750s, the major collieries in the region had become reliant on the waggonway to move their coal from pit head to loading staith. In fact, it is hard to see how an increased production would have been possible using just road transport.

The growth of the coal trade, so vital to the economy of the Tyne and Wear region, was influenced by more than just the development of the waggonway. Early in the eighteenth century, an effective steam engine was introduced – the Newcomen engine – which was powerful enough to pump out some of the drowned shafts near the Tyne and allowed the exploitation of deeper seams. But the investment now necessary for the sinking of deep pits, including pumping engines and the provision of a waggonway, was so large that reliable, large scale production was essential and here again the advantages of the waggonway over the road were of crucial importance.

An immense benefit to the coal-merchants

Noted by Lord Guildford, 1676, with some exaggeration.

'When men have pieces of ground between a colliery and the river, they will sell leave to lead coals over their ground, and so dear, that the owner of a rood of ground will expect £20 per annum for the leave. The manner of the carriage is by laying rails of timber from the colliery down to the river exactly straight and parallel, and bulky carts are made with four rowlets [flanged wheels] fitting these rails, whereby the carriage is so easy, that one horse will draw down four or five chaldrons of coals, and is an immense benefit to the coal-merchants.'

Waggonway Winters

From the *Newcastle Journal*, 26 January, 1740.

Newcastle, Jan 16

The Coal Owners of Durham and Northumberland have been at very great Expense in clearing their Waggon-Ways of Snows, and still continue to employ great Numbers of poor People in that Work, who are by the Severity of the Weather deprived of following any other Employment. By these means the labouring People in this neighbourhood have the happiness to enjoy the Blessing of Plenty; whilst others in several Parts of this Island are (by all Accounts) starving for want of Subsistence. There are already above 600 Coal-Carriages at Work, and others are going to work daily; so that if this Weather continues, the several Staithes will be well replenish'd with Coals, ready to supply the Wants of the Necessitous when the frost breaks up, and the City of London and other Places will be well supply'd in their greatest Scarcity at the usual Rates; for though Coals are now selling from 19 to 20s. per Chaldron in this Town from the neighbouring Land sale Collieries, the Coal-Owners are selling theirs, of a much superior Quality, at the usual prices, being about 2d. per Bushel, tho' the same Bushel is now retailed in London for Half a Crown.

A rare coloured print of a Tyneside colliery, c.1800. The steam engine drains the pit, a horse gin raises the coal in wicker 'corves' whilst the waggons are loaded for the long drop to the river.

The Newcastle Road

There was a broad pattern to the growth of the waggonways serving the Tyne. Most of those which opened before 1750 led to the south bank of the river, whereas the majority built in the following fifty years went to the north. This was due to a combination of circumstances. The Durham pits had rich seams of coal, relatively close to the surface but often a long distance from the river; production was cheap but road transport expensive and difficult. In 1712, for example, the costings for transport were calculated for the Tanfield Moor Colliery. Not only could almost four times as much coal be moved by waggonway than by road, but it would cost far less per ton and potentially increase the profits of the pits nearly ten fold. This scale of economy was spectacular – the development of the waggonway had a crucial effect on the viability of this part of the coalfield.

The pits on the north side of the Tyne were typically much closer to the river but were often either drowned out or with exhausted top seams. Although the Newcomen engine could bring better drainage and allow for lower seams to be exploited, many of the pits had to be extremely deep, often with problems with water and gas, so that their production costs were high and the advantages of their shorter waggonway less marked. However, the balance of economics began to change during the second half of the eighteenth century. Greater demand, better engines, increased co-opera-tion between the owners, and a greater availability of finance made it worthwhile to invest in deep mining to exploit the excellent seams found particularly to the north and east of Newcastle. The Tyne Bridge blocked access to ships upstream, but downstream there was the added advantage that the eastern pits could send their coal directly into the colliers, avoiding the expense and breakage of using keels. Sinking and production costs were still high however

The stone arches of the Tyne Bridge blocked collier traffic upstream. John Brand's **History of Newcastle**, *1789, shows a coal waggon descending to the river, the driver sitting on the brake lever. Rather appropriately this site would form the south end of the High Level Bridge 60 years later.*

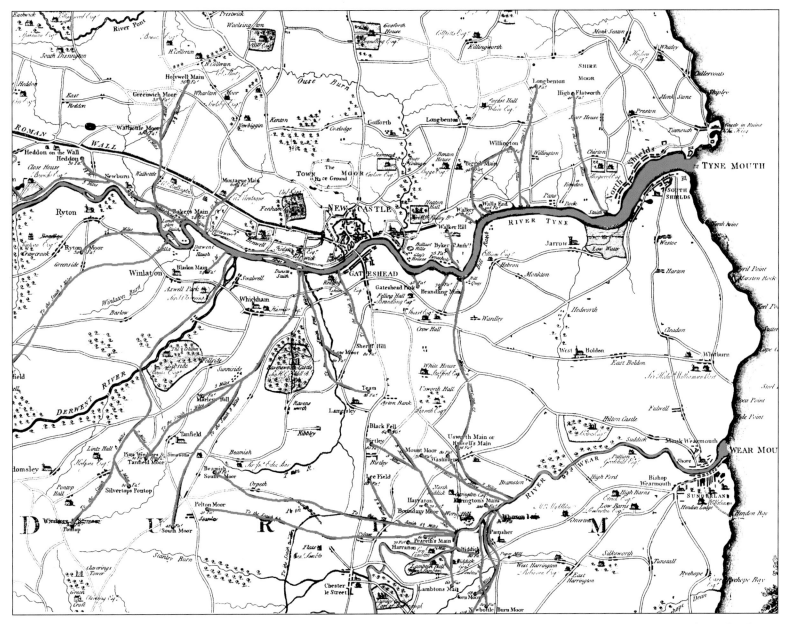

Gibson's map of 1787, with the waggonways emphasised in red. The routes north of the Tyne will soon be greatly expanded, those to the south are already long and extensive. On the Wear, suitable river banks are restricted, concentrating the staiths – Sunderland will not be reached by a colliery waggonway until 1812.

and worthwhile only if accompanied by a greatly increased tonnage of quality coal. Again, the capacity of the waggonway and its less damaging effect on the large coal was crucial.

It has been estimated that by 1800 there were perhaps 150 route miles of waggonway in the North East and that this represented half the mileage of the country as a whole. The waggonway could be found in many parts of Britain, particularly in the coal-producing areas of northern England, the Midlands and Wales. But it was best known around Tyneside and Wearside, and the 'Newcastle Road' became a nationally-recognised name for the waggonway. Visitors commented on the strange sight of the waggons as they rolled downhill, the driver casually sitting on top with horse following behind and the characteristic heavy rumble of the wheels as they rolled over the wood rails.

At most collieries the traffic might seem quite light. Many in the first half of the eighteenth century would see less than 100 waggons a day using the line, but the largest collieries produced very heavy traffic – Tanfield saw over 900 waggon movements each day and it was this scale of usage that could justify what seemed to be an immense investment in its rail systems. The multitude of main lines and branches left their mark over much of the Tyne and the Wear area. The railway had developed into an industry in its own right with thousands of waggons, horses, drivers and specialised trackworkers.

The growth of the waggonway had been spectacular in the last half of the eighteenth century – and without competition. Elsewhere in the country, many of the waggonways were used to join the collieries to the local canal systems. The North East had no usable waterways except for the Tyne and Wear. There were various schemes for canals in the later eighteenth century, but the landscape of the region, with its hills and deep denes, meant that the projects were expensive. Local landowners made so much money from waggonway wayleaves that they had little interest in support-

A coal certificate of c.1800 shows the waggons unloading down the 'spouts' to a keel and collier. A door beneath the waggon dropped to release the coal.

ing canals, colliery owners preferred the control they could maintain by having their own lines and the rail system was sufficiently developed that the attraction of permanently fixed waterways was minimal. This would be one of the very few industrialised areas of Britain that did not adopt the canal, concentrating its attention on the improvement of the railway. By 1800, over three million tons of coal were being produced in Durham and Northumberland each year. With its associated industries and great collier fleets, it was the lynchpin of the local economy – it is inconceivable that such a scale of production could have developed using road transport alone.

The Unequalled Arch

Just a few miles from the centre of Newcastle stands a monument, not just to the waggonway, but to the whole development of the Industrial Revolution. In its day, nearly 300 years ago, it was famous, now it receives surprisingly few visits, yet it should be considered as one of the glories of the region, as impressive and beautiful as it is important.

Tanfield, or Causey, Arch lies just to the north of Stanley, a stone's throw from Beamish Museum. Its story tells not only of a great feat of civil engineering, but of the personal conflicts and ambitions that affected the growth of the waggonway in the North East. When the Tanfield route was planned in 1723, its advantages were not just that it was shorter and more level than its predecessor, but that it would no longer cross the land of the rector of Whickham causing regular arguments about the wayleave charges: 'By this new way you would miss the Rector, and so not lye at the mercy of every New one.' The long waggonway and the civil engineering it required was extremely expensive – the reason it could be afforded was because it was built by a partnership of some of the biggest landowners and businessmen of the area – the 'Grand Allies'. The line was built to exploit collieries at Causey and Tanfield, leased out to two of the partners. The major problem was the crossing of the Causey Burn, which, like so many streams in the region, had cut itself a very steep-sided dene. It was not possible to take a waggonway down this abrupt incline and up the other side, so it would have to be bridged not once but twice to maintain a reasonable gradient.

For the first crossing to the south, a stone bridge was built to span the valley. Opened in the summer of 1725, it collapsed almost straight away. Undeterred, if surely rather shaken, the Allies immediately started a new bridge which was completed after rather more than a year at a cost of over £2000. The builder was Ralph Wood, sometimes described as a 'country mason' but more an engineer. He put up the most spectacular structure, a single semi-elliptical arch with a span of 105 feet – for 30 years the longest single span of any bridge in Britain – and a deck some 80 feet above the burn, with massive retaining walls to the approaches.

A very different solution was found for the second crossing, a few hundred yards downstream. The dene here was much wider so a bridge would be prohibitively expensive. Instead an enormous

Detail from a late eighteenth century watercolour of Tanfield Arch by Robert Johnson. Already the great retaining walls are collapsing and the heavier traffic diverted.

Andy Guy

Tanfield Arch, the greatest monument to the waggonway age, as it is today. Visitors can walk over the bridge and embankment, or use the dramatic and very attractive riverside path.

Britain since Roman times. Even now they are perhaps the most significant remains of the waggonway age, more important because they were so early. Nor was it just their construction that had such impact. When the railway was little known in the rest of the country, here was a grand project of scale, beauty and ambition that was justified by taking two lines of wooden tracks across a valley to ease the gradients. It led to a realisation that the waggonway was to be a significant player in transport, that its advantages could repay what was a huge private investment, that the coal trade and the railway were to be major components of the accelerating Industrial Revolution.

Landslips damaged the approaches to the bridge only a few years after its completion – an alternate route opened that took much of the heavier traffic, but it remained in use for much of the rest of the eighteenth century. It slowly deteriorated for nearly 200 years until restored by Durham County Council during the 1970s and 1980s. The embankment was used until the whole route was closed in 1962, but reopened as the present preserved Tanfield Railway. As such it can claim to be the oldest working line in the world.

earth embankment was constructed to fill in the valley, with a conduit taking the burn beneath. It is taken for granted now that huge quantities of earth can be moved relatively easily – we have the machines for it. Then it was by spade and cart, waggon and barrow; as remarkable a feat as the famous arch.

Each of these crossings alone was deeply impressive; together they had a strong effect on the people of the time. It is likely that no similar feats of civil engineering had been tried on this scale in

An Immense Expense

Once a colliery decided to build a waggonway it had two major decisions to make. What was the best route, and could they gain permission to cross the ground?

The perfect line was as short as possible and descended gently from the pit to the staith, so that one horse could take the loaded waggon downhill and bring the empty back up. If the descent was too steep there could be serious problems with the full waggon running out of control and the horse might have difficulty returning the empty. A loose rule was developed by the 1750s that the gradient should certainly not be more than one in ten down from the pit and preferably much less. More importantly, there should be the absolute minimum incline for the full waggons to be pulled uphill, to avoid the time-consuming and expensive process of hitching on additional horses as 'helpers-up'. The horse has a very limited level of power and stamina. The waggonway had to be planned with those restrictions in mind. In the long term it could be economic to grade the line with cuttings, embankments and bridges to maintain the most effective level, as at Tanfield Arch, and this was commonly necessary in the North East, which was dominated by hills, by the rivers Team and Derwent south of the Tyne, and by a series of deep denes to its north.

Coal Waggon

With the best route selected, the next problem was to arrange permission from the land owners for the line to cross their fields. This would take the form of a 'wayleave agreement', by which the owner was typically paid a 'certain rent' due every year for the right to build and use the waggonway, plus an extra charge depending on how many tons of coal were taken across. As the possible routes were very limited, the landowners enjoyed considerable negotiating power, and so these wayleave charges could be extremely high – a major source of income for them and a considerable expense to the colliery.

The situation could become more complicated. If the landowner had competing collieries it might be in his best interests to block access or even to buy up land essential to the route. This was one reason for the foundation of a partnership of coal and landowners, the 'Grand Allies' to combine their wayleave powers, deny them to others and confound their enemies.

The route of a waggonway was seldom a foregone conclusion. It depended on a delicate balance of interest: between the position of the pit for the highest production, the geography of the land with the expenses necessary to form the best gradient, and the permission and charges of the wayleave owners. Much of the history of the waggonway in the North East is dominated by these changing forces. Where we usually think of the railway as a 'permanent way', it was not really so until well into the nineteenth century. During the preceding 200 years, the local waggonways often changed their routes to take into account worked-out pits, easier gradients or cheaper wayleaves.

Once the route and wayleaves were agreed, the colliery engineer, or 'viewer', laid out the line and the waggonway wrights could start construction. If cuts and embankments were necessary, the earth removed from one could be used to build up the other and, if possible, allowed to settle and consolidate for a year. Where bridges were necessary, they were generally made of timber for cheapness – Tanfield Arch was a remarkable exception.

The trackbed itself needed careful preparation if it was to last. Without proper drainage it would become boggy and soft, disrupting and rotting the wooden track so that, in this region, it was usual to dig drainage gutters to either side. Between these were laid the ballast, not the hard crushed rock used today, but more often a combination of gash stone, ash, cinders and the small coal that was worthless to the colliery. Wooden sleepers were put down, roughly shaped but preferably of oak for long life, and the rails pegged to them with wooden 'nails'. A layer of fine ballast was laid over the sleepers to form a solid and even track for the horses and protect the sleepers from damage from the horses' hooves, with other material packed under the rails to spread the load and firm them up so that they barely appeared to rise above the surface. On each side of the tracks the ballast was continued to make a firm pathway for the waggon-men to walk alongside, making a total width of perhaps 14 feet for a single track, bounded by fencing.

Most of the early wood waggonways were single with passing places. As traffic increased, the busier collieries were building twin

An Emergency Waggonway

From *Coals on rails, or the reason of my Wrighting*, the autobiography of waggonway wright Anthony Errington.

c.1809: 'The Hollihill pit had worked sometime as Land Sale for John Grase. John Straker and John Brandling had 500 Chalder of Coals at the pit. The railway was taken up but these Coals was Sold to go to Scotland. I had to begin on the Monday morning with 12 hands and lay down 345 yards of railway, which was done of the Wednesday at 4 o'clock and 3 Chaldern of Coals shipped that Evening. The Wager of 20 guineas that the Ship Should have the Coals on the Wednesday was bet by Straker. We was rewarded with One hauf Barrel of Ale and Cheas and Bread that evening.'

Fawdon Staith from Wallsend. Tyne & Wear Museums

The quintessential view of the 'Newcastle Road'. The chaldron waggon runs on flanged wheels and is fitted with a shovel and 'convoy' or brake. Between the wooden rails the sleepers are covered to give a smooth surface for the horse and driver. This watercolour was painted about 1800 by the leading colliery viewer of his day, John Buddle, 'King of the Coal Trade'. A replica of the waggon can be seen at Beamish Museum.

tracks, one a heavily constructed 'main way' for the loaded waggons and the other a 'bye way' for the returning empties, which
could be more lightly built and less well graded. The costs were
highly variable, depending on the number of tracks
and the engineering work necessary, but were substantial, especially for the supply of prepared
woodwork and costs increased steadily throughout
the eighteenth century.

Effective though the waggonway was,
it had the problem of a less than ideal
track material. Wood is relatively soft,
particularly when wet, and could quickly
develop depressions on the bearing surface from the pressure of the waggon
wheels, leading to an unevenness that
greatly increased friction. Nor is it wear resistant or
long-lasting, so the maintenance costs could be very high. With
average traffic, the rails of the main way might last three years, but
if usage was really heavy their life might be no more than a year.
Sleepers could last longer but inevitably suffered damage from the
continual replacement of the rail pins and wear from the horses'
feet as the thin ballast wore through.

A partial solution was to nail a 'sacrificial' top rail to the bottom rail, a device commonly used on the main ways from the mid-
eighteenth century. This could then easily be replaced without dis-
turbing the whole section and its added height meant that the
sleepers could be better protected by a deeper layer of ballast.
Excessive wear remained a problem on curves and on the steeper
drops where ash and cinders might have been spread to help in
braking. Towards the end of the century, thin iron plates were occasionally nailed to the top rail to give longer service. It was an indi-
cation that the days of the wooden waggonway were coming to an
end.

WOODEN WAGGONWAY 1765

A view of a Tyneside waggon in Voyages Métallurgiques *by Gabriel Jars,
showing the iron hooks that held the brake lever on or off. Although waggonways were used on the continent they were rarely as extensive or as
heavily used as those in the North East and their description was often cir-
culated abroad.*

The Timber Trackway at Lambton D Pit

Ian Ayris

In the mid 1990s one of the most important archaeological sites relating to the development of the railway was discovered lying under metres of coal waste on the site of the former Lambton Cokeworks near Fencehouses in the City of Sunderland. Hidden for over 150 years, the remains of a timber railway, dating from the last years of the eighteenth century and the early years of the nineteenth century, were painstakingly excavated by archaeologists. The site had been that of the Lambton D Pit, a mine opened out between 1789 and 1791. The excavation uncovered substantial remains of both brick- and stone-built engine and boiler houses, including specific features such as the base for a haystack boiler, potentially dating from 1802, ash pits, and loading ramps. However, the main interest lay in what proved to be the unearthing of the largest and most complete timber waggonway ever excavated in this country. Prior to this, archaeological evidence of early waggonways was based on only three comparably minor discoveries. As a consequence, Lambton D was a remarkably important site.

In total, some 150 metres of surviving timber trackway was found – sections of four substantially complete tracks, together with ground impressions and fragmentary remains of a further six tracks, all of which formed a complex of lines extending to and from the former pit, carrying coal away to the River Wear. This was the best opportunity yet to study the way in which timber railways were built.

The rails were cut from oak tree boles in a variety of lengths up to 3.30m, approximately 12-13 cm square and laid at a gauge of 1.3m or 4ft 3in. The rails were drilled and pegged with wooden 'nails' to timber sleepers, which were themselves very roughly cut sections of oak tree branches up to 2m long. In places there were also timber check rails which prevented waggons from veering off

Ian Ayris

Sleepers, timber rails and the immovable 'points' at Lambton D.

the track on bends. Perhaps the most intriguing aspects were two sets of primitive 'points' where lines interconnected. With no moving parts, the points seemed to have worked largely by dint of physically pushing waggons across the rails. It is assumed that the work of moving the full and empty waggons around the pit yard and on to the main Lambton Waggonway was done by horses, but strangely no evidence of horses was found at the site – not even a nail from a horse-shoe. What was striking, however, was the extent to which the formation of the track and the materials used were almost identical to a description of a Tyneside waggonway written by Gabriel Jars in 1765 (see page 20).

Without doubt, the most remarkable aspect of the whole site was the way in which the wood had survived. The timber rails had probably last been used in the 1830s when they had been overlaid with a bed of ash and coal waste upon which a new iron railway had been set out. At the end of archaeological investigation the timber was once again covered up and protected under layers of clay. One of the most exciting industrial archaeological sites in the region, which afforded a glimpse into the eighteenth century development of the railway, lies once again buried beneath the soil.

An aerial view of the extensive trackwork at Lambton. Before this excavation, only fragments of early wooden waggonway had been discovered.

On the Right Track

Towards the end of the eighteenth century, the waggonway saw the most fundamental improvement in track for almost 200 years. The iron rail had been enthusiastically adopted elsewhere in the country, particularly in the Midlands and Wales where cast iron was relatively cheap and readily available. It was not used in this region until 1797 when the Lawson Main Colliery ordered it for part of the waggonway. Iron had the advantages of long life, perhaps ten years or more, and low upkeep compared to wood, with the added benefit of a good scrap value even when worn out, but, more important, it was a far more efficient surface for the wheels. It was estimated at the time that a horse could pull between 30 and 100 per cent more weight on this smooth, hard new track so that it might now take two or even three waggons at a time instead of one, yet the maintenance costs could be halved at the same time. The major drawback was the great initial cost of the new lines, which needed expensive iron rails with chairs mounted on stone sleeper blocks sunk into the ground, requiring the relaying of the whole waggonway.

Once the principle was seen to be so effective, it quickly took over from the wood waggonway. Between 1810 and 1830 nearly all the region's major lines were converted and all but the most modest new waggonways constructed with iron from the beginning. Apart

The 'L' shaped plate rail was commonly used elsewhere in Britain. The wheel was plain, the rail flanged and almost flush with the ground.

The edge rail, preferred in the North East – a flanged wheel on a raised flat rail, much as modern track is today.

One of the inclines at the Bowes Railway, near Gateshead, now the only place to see the operation of standard gauge cable-haulage, a power system that would outlive the steam locomotive.

from sidings and odd branch lines, wooden rails had become redundant.

The North East had not adopted the design of iron rail that was popular in many other parts of the country. Elsewhere, the 'ledge' or 'plate' rail was commonly used, L-shaped so that the wheel itself no longer needed a flange to follow the track. Relatively cheap and easy to lay, it added the possibility of allowing carriages of the right gauge to use either road or rail without the need for trans-shipment. It had been invented by a local man, John Curr from Pontop, but ironically it was least popular in his home area and its only major user locally was Wylam Colliery.

The North East preferred the edge rail, like the wooden ones it had replaced, with a smooth top and the flange on the wheel and in principle much like the ones used today. This was an important preference for, as the horse waggonway developed into the mechanically-powered railway, the edge rail worked the best – the plate rail became a technical dead-end. The emerging railway engineers of the North East were to have a head start.

At this same period, the first of the mechanical improvements was seen in the region. The balanced incline or self-acting plane was fundamentally a simple device that had been known for some time. It worked on the principle that if the slope was sufficient the weight of a number of loaded waggons going downhill could be used to pull another set of empties back up on a parallel track. All that was needed was a rope to connect them, travelling round a drum at the top, which could be braked if necessary.

Although the lines had already been graded to allow, where possible, a waggon to go some of the way down by gravity, each one still needed a driver to brake it and a horse attached to bring it back. With the self-acting incline, horses and drivers could be dispensed with for whole sets of waggons and the power source was free and inexhaustible. Not only that but waggonways could be planned to use steeper descents and many routes were rebuilt to take advantage of them. Where an incline had been a problem, it could now be an advantage – in modern terms here was a model of an economical, energy efficient and sustainable transport system.

Quite when the balanced plane was first used in the region is not known, but it was certainly by 1784, when the French traveller Faujaus de Saint-Fond observed that on Tyneside: '... when the local circumstances have permitted, the weight of the load, and the accelerated movement have been combined in such a manner that files of loaded waggons run down the inclined plane and at the same time cause the empty waggons to reascend without the assistance of horses, along another road parallel to the first'. The earliest recorded location we have is at Benwell in 1798, used in conjunction with iron rails. This incorporated an unusual and rather ingenious variation in that it used the weight of a chain to store the power of the loaded waggons. As the waggons went downhill, they raised a heavy chain in the pit shaft. When the waggons reached the bottom they were released, empties attached and as the chain dropped down the shaft again under its own weight, it pulled up the waggons. This arrangement would not prove popular, but the self-acting plane in general became widespread in the North East and stayed in use right throughout and beyond the era of the steam locomotive.

The same could be said of another waggonway development of the period. Although many of the problems of downhill running had been solved, there was still that of getting loaded waggons uphill. The answer again was simple enough – to pull them up with a stationary steam engine. The first is believed to have been used on the Urpeth Waggonway, near Chester-le-Street, in 1809 and, as engines of increasing power and less cost were developed, this cable haulage system also became a familiar feature in the region.

Powered haulage and the balanced plane were very significant evolutions of the waggonway system, both in the Northern Coalfield and in other parts of Britain. As a way of overcoming the problem of gradient, they could be extremely effective, but their uses were usually restricted by their reliance on being tethered to a cable, their need for individual machines on each stretch of track

Picton Main pit, c.1825, showing the cable rollers, horse haulage and a waggon being re-axled. Loading certificates often advertised the technical advances of the colliery.

Steam haulage

From Sykes, *Remarkable Events*

May 17, 1809

The opening of the waggon-way from Bewicke main to the river Tyne took place, on which occasion every road leading to it was crowded with passengers at an early hour, and before eleven o'clock, about 10,000 people were assembled. About this time four waggons of small coals were brought up the first plane by the steam engine, to the great admiration of the spectators, but owing to some little difficulties which often occur in new machinery, the four waggons of best coals, intended for the Tyne, did not start till a much later hour. As soon as the waggons reached the summit of the second and highest plane, up which they went with surprising velocity and regularity, the British flag was hoisted at Ayton cottage, and announced by a discharge of six pieces of cannon, which were answered by an equal number from the Ann and Isabella, his majesty's armed ship on the Tyne, and from Deptford-house, the residence of Mr Cooke. Immediately on the waggons reaching the first plane, about 400 gentlemen sat down to dinner, in a tent fitted up for the occasion. An excellent military band attended. In the evening, in order to prove the excellence of the level railway, six men, without horses, took with the greatest ease four laden waggons, with each ten men on the top, from Ayton cottage to the Tyne; and the first coals being put on board the Ann and Isabella, the same was announced by discharges of artillery as before.

and on the immediate topography being suitable; for longer distances and flatter tracks the horse remained both the answer and the problem. Its mechanical replacement would transform the railway from local waggonways to a national and international system. It would be its single most important development and it would take place in the North East.

The top of the self-acting plane at Church Pit, Wallsend. The connecting wheel is in the roof space of the building, through which, at right angles, runs the Killingworth waggonway. This 1838 watercolour is by the great artist of the Northern Coalfield, Thomas Hair.

The Pioneers of Steam

It is a common misapprehension that George Stephenson invented the steam locomotive. He might have achieved many things but this was certainly not one of them, nor was the locomotive first seen in the North East. It was the brainchild of a brilliant Cornish engineer, Richard Trevithick, who had patented the high pressure steam engine.

RICHARD TREVITHICK

The Newcomen steam engines that had initiated so much growth in the coalfields were useful but desperately short of power and efficiency. Both were greatly increased by the improvements made by James Watt towards the end of the eighteenth century, and his engine would be the standard design for slow-speed work for something like a hundred years. But Watt insisted on the use of only low steam pressures, often of just a few pounds per square inch, with a separate condenser to add vacuum pressure, which meant that his machines had to be massive affairs to achieve the necessary power.

Trevithick, the 'Captain' or engineer of mineral mines in Cornwall, had a different solution. By using steam at up to 50psi, he not only greatly increased the power in relation to the engine weight but he also could afford to get rid of the cumbersome condenser and the huge boilers. For the first time it was possible to have an effective portable engine. A man of great ingenuity and

Beamish

imagination, he very quickly grasped its potential and at the end of 1801 he was testing a steam road carriage. The initial trials were very promising but were followed by disaster. As he and his friends celebrated in the local pub, the unattended fire in the boiler overheated the carriage and it was burnt to a crisp. It was the kind of tragic comedy that would follow Trevithick throughout his life.

He was not yet deterred, however. The following year he went to London and took out a patent for his high pressure engine, including in it the specific use for carriages. He built another example which he tested around the northern edge of the city but, although it worked well in principle, it proved too difficult to control in the streets and suffered from the uneven surface, leading Trevithick to abandon development of the steam road carriage. The obvious next step was to try the idea on the waggonways, where steering was not a problem , friction was much less and the 'road' was smooth.

Quite how and by whom that first railway locomotive was built is surprisingly uncertain. In a letter of August 1802, Trevithick casually mentioned that 'The Dale Co. have began a carriage at their own cost for the real-roads and is forcing it with all expedition'. The Company was at Coalbrookdale, the present site of the Ironbridge Gorge Museum, but there are no details surviving of the trials or if they had any success – the engine may have been aban-

The working replica of the presumed Coalbrookdale locomotive. The engine is tiny, dwarfed by its great flywheel, but works on the plate rails surprisingly well. Firebox, chimney, cylinder and slides all struggle for space at one end – a fireman's nightmare.

doned without doing any real work. An 1803 drawing of a 'Tram engine' for use on plate rails does exist and this may well represent the Coalbrookdale locomotive, but it is still not at all clear who made the detailed design. The Ironbridge Museum runs a working replica based on this drawing.

Much more is known about the next engine. Trevithick had made some of his high pressure stationary engines for the Penydarren ironworks at Merthyr Tydfil. Its owner, Samuel Homfray, bet another local ironfounder that one of the engines could be used on the waggonway to take down ten tons of iron and return with the empty waggons. The experiments in the spring of 1804 were successful to a degree, but there was a problem in that the weight of the locomotive broke the iron plate rails and the engine was removed from the waggonway to work in the foundry.

The world's third locomotive was built in the North East. Trevithick wrote in January 1805 that he would, 'go to Newcastle-upon-Tyne in about four weeks ... I expect that there are some of the travelling engines at work at Newcastle.' His agent in the region was John Whinfield of Gateshead, who joined forces with local man, John Steele, to make a locomotive they hoped would sell to the Wylam Colliery waggonway. Steele was a fascinating man. Born near Pontop, he had lost a leg in an accident on the line when young, but had proved to be an excellent mechanic. He had gone to work for Trevithick and was closely involved with the Penydarren experiments, so was a natural choice to introduce the locomotive to his native area. Two major detailed drawings survive of the Gateshead engine; they suggest that both Trevithick and Steele were responsible for the design, which is known to have been demonstrated in the grounds of Whinfield's works along Pipewellgate in the summer of 1805.

The drawings show an engine with typical features of these early Trevithick locomotives. There is only one cylinder, working horizontally and driving a huge flywheel whose momentum was essential to prevent the piston being caught at dead centre. Drive was taken by gears to the wheels and the cast iron boiler was a compact design which used a U-shaped flue to give the maximum heating area, so the firebox was alongside the chimney. What is significant is that it was working on wooden edge rails, an essential feature for this region, whereas his previous engines had been for flanged plate rails.

Christopher Blackett, owner of Wylam colliery, decided not to

The 'Penydarren' replica, based on the drawings for the Gateshead engine but on a reduced gauge and fitted for plate rails. Still using a flywheel and gearing but with the single horizontal cylinder placed at the other end of the boiler.

Newcastle Courant, *22 October 1803*

take the engine. Quite why is uncertain, but the most likely reason is that it had proved unsuitable for the wooden rails, although the test site at Pipewellgate was extremely congested and would not have shown off this type of locomotive at all well. The engine spent the rest of its life blowing the foundry and it lasted there for over 60 years but sadly was not preserved. It would have been the sole surviving Trevithick 'travelling engine' for the railway and the world's oldest surviving locomotive.

There are no drawings of the Penydarren locomotive, so that when a working replica was constructed it was decided to base it on the Gateshead drawings, adapted for different dimensions and for plate rather than edge rail, but it does mean that the type can be seen (presently, at the National Railway Museum) and a strong impression given of what it was like when it was demonstrated at Pipewellgate.

Trevithick made one final attempt to interest the public in his steam locomotive. In 1808 he built a circular demonstration track in north London, where he charged people to see and travel on his new design, *Catch Me Who Can*. As an attraction it failed to pay. When the engine was derailed, he gave up and dismantled the show. He would not build another, but he did have the opportunity. Blackett of Wylam had replaced his wood waggonway with a new iron plate rail track and, in 1809, asked Trevithick to build a locomotive for it. But the inventor had had enough and was following other interests, '… if I had been in your neighbourhood I should have no objection to make an engine of this kind for you but being at such a distance and my time fully occupied with other business therefore must decline engaging this job.'

His decision was unfortunate. As well as being the first passenger engine, if the surviving sketches of *Catch Me* are at all accurate it was a small, fast engine with the drive going directly from the vertical piston rod to the rear wheels via a connecting rod, dispensing with all the gears and flywheel. Its design was very advanced

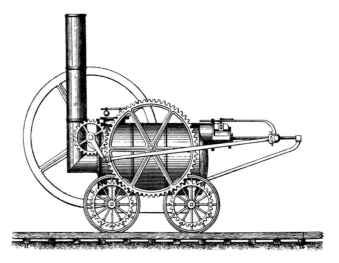

The Trevithick Gateshead engine, the first edge-rail locomotive.

and nothing like it would be seen until the Rainhill Trials over twenty years later. Had Trevithick taken up Blackett's offer and developed his engines for the North East it is likely that the history of the locomotive would have taken a very different course. But it was not to be, and as far as we know there were no more trials for three years.

JOHN BLENKINSOP AND MATTHEW MURRAY

In 1811 a colliery viewer called John Blenkinsop patented a system where an engine drove a cogged wheel along a matching toothed or rack rail, much as mountain railways are worked today. The locomotive was built by Fenton, Murray and Wood of Leeds but it is believed that the engine design itself was by its engineer, Matthew Murray. He made a crucial breakthrough in fitting twin cylinders instead of Trevithick's single, giving more available power, a smoother action and, with four power strokes now possible, solving the problem of the dead centre stall. His arrangement of vertical cylinders in the centre line of the boiler top, with slide bar motion and connecting rods, would be the basis for most general designs of locomotive for the next 15 years.

Two engines were ready by June 1812 and the system was opened at the Middleton Colliery near Leeds, where Blenkinsop was the viewer. Despite the inevitable teething problems and the expense of the special rack rails, it was judged a great success and was widely publicised. For the first time the steam locomotive was in regular work and demonstrating that it could be a realistic alternative to the horse. Where Trevithick had shown that the locomotive was possible, it was Blenkinsop and Murray who proved it could be practical.

John Blenkinsop was born in 1783 at Low Heworth, just east of Gateshead, where his family had been stone masons for at least two generations. John was apprenticed to Thomas Barnes, the greatest colliery viewer and technical innovator of his day and then, after

Barnes' death in 1801, to his successor, John Straker of Felling Hall. The owner of the local pits was Charles Brandling, who also held the Middleton Colliery on the outskirts of Leeds, and it was to there that Blenkinsop was appointed viewer in 1808. He remained in Leeds until his death but often visited his home area and kept in close contact with the local viewers, sometimes acting as a consultant to Brandling's Tyneside collieries. Unmarried, he died in 1831 at the age of 47, possibly as a result of injuries sustained six years before during a rescue attempt at Brandling's pit in Gosforth. He deserves much more recognition, not least in his native North East. Not only did he produce the first practical locomotive system, but he sold it to the Orrell Colliery near Wigan, to Tyneside, possibly to a Welsh pit and demonstrated it to visiting European royalty, including the future Czar of Russia. The first

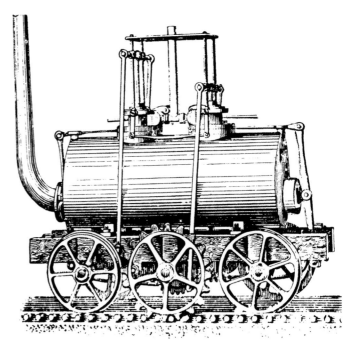

The Blenkinsop rack system and Murray's engine. The breakthrough design, twin cylinders dispensing with the flywheel and increasing power.

locomotives on the continent would be two Blenkinsop rack engines built in Prussia. His was the breakthrough that Trevithick had failed to achieve.

The origins of Matthew Murray are rather more obscure. It is said that he was born at Newcastle in 1765, but there seems no firm evidence of this and it is possible that he actually came from the Scottish Borders. He certainly spent at least some of his youth in the North East, for he married a Whickham girl, Mary Thompson, at Gateshead in 1785. He subsequently worked in the Stockton-Darlington area where he learned the new techniques of spinning flax mechanically, a knowledge that was to prove very useful when he moved down to Leeds soon after. A brilliant mechanic and engineer, he became the technical force behind the great engineering firm of Fenton, Murray and Wood, acknowledged at the time as the main competitor to Boulton and Watt. Murray, who died in 1826, should have been one of the leaders of the locomotive revolution but his experience with the Blenkinsop engines convinced him that they were too difficult and demanding to build for profit compared to the market for standard stationary engines; as a result the company refused further requests to make locomotives until the 1830s.

The success of the Middleton trials of 1812 stimulated a remarkable series of experiments over the next three years, nearly all of which were to take place in the North East. Blenkinsop actively marketed his system, it was well covered in the press and he had contacts in the area. It was not surprising that one of the Newcastle collieries, the Kenton and Coxlodge, decided to try it out. They had a nearly new iron railway that went from west Gosforth, crossed the Ouseburn near Heaton then headed south to join up with the Bigges Main wooden waggonway and down to staiths at Wallsend. Blenkinsop promised the viewer, John Watson, that installing his system could potentially save the colliery a fortune.

The figures he calculated were startling, so much so that he felt bound to warn that 'you will be very much astonished at the savings …' and it is worth looking at them as they explain why the collieries were to be so interested in the new locomotives. The Napoleonic Wars had led to a massive increase in the cost of maintaining horses, with feedstuffs at record prices. The locomotive might not only cut their numbers but it could be 'fed' on coal. At the Kenton and Coxlodge waggonway the estimate was over £4,000 to replace one side of the rails with his special toothed rack. The seven engines necessary to move the coal five and a half miles to the staiths would be a further £2,100. Even assuming that the costs of keeping horses would not 'continue so expensive' as the present rate of £78 a year each, but could be reasonably calculated to be £50, their annual total cost was still nearly £9,500. However, if locomotives were substituted, the expenditure would plummet to less than £1,500 a year, equivalent to a drop in the cost of transporting a chaldron of coals from over 30p to less than 5p.

Matthew Murray's estimates were considerably more conservative, but even then the savings were to be more than £2,000 a year.

He said, '… the engines themselves answer much beyond our expectations and which I have no doubt in saying is the most valuable improvement to the colliery business that has been made these 50 years, particularly for pits that are situated a considerable distance from the sea and where the expenses of horse and keep is a considerable draw back from the profits of the coals.' By a handy coincidence this was of course exactly the situation of the Kenton and Coxlodge.

The only view of a Blenkinsop of the Kenton & Coxlodge Colliery, on a coal certificate of c.1815. But this was only a marketing ploy. The system was not actually completed as the essential cog rails were never laid down to the staiths.

Even if the figures were treated with some caution, potential savings could revolutionise the economy of the coalfield. Watson ordered three engines from Matthew Murray and initially arranged for just under two miles of the waggonway to be converted to rack rail, from the Jubilee Pit (following the line of the present Jubilee Road) to the Ouseburn bridge at Haddrick's Mill. It opened in September 1813 to a great crowd of spectators, who saw the first engine, *Lord Wellington*, move off with 16 full waggons. The locomotive was finally at work in the North East.

WILLIAM CHAPMAN

Reasonably successful though the rack system was, it was not without competition. In March 1813 Blenkinsop, had written to John Watson, 'Chapman's plan is only a mechanical larceny – I will thank you for a description of it, if you know his scheme.' William Chapman and his brother had patented an alternative to the rack railway. In their design, a chain laid down the centre of the track was taken up by the engine and driven round a drum to pull the locomotive forward, rather like a travelling winch. While the Blenkinsop rack rails were being laid down at Coxlodge, Chapman's chains were being prepared on the nearby Heaton Colliery waggonway. His locomotive, built by the Butterley Company of Derbyshire, was ready for its tests by the end of October. It was not to prove very successful, undergoing months of modifications without doing any real practical work. The

An ingenious experiment

From the *Newcastle Courant* 4 September 1813

'On Thursday last, an ingenious and highly interesting experiment was performed, in the presence of a vast concourse of spectators, on the rail-way leading from the collieries of Kenton and Coxlodge, near this town, by the application of a steam engine, constructed by Fenton, Murray and Wood, of Leeds, under the direction of Mr John Blenkinsop, the patentee, for the purpose of drawing the coal-waggons. The machine in question is simply a steam engine of four horses power, so constructed, that, by the operating aid of cranks, which turn a cogged-wheel, (iron cogs being placed on one side of the rail-way) a considerable power of motion is given to the machine,—a power so considerable, indeed, that when the machine is but lightly loaded, it can be propelled at the rate of ten miles per hour… we feel complete satisfaction at the complete success that has attended the experiment in this quarter. And much praise we conceive is due to the spirited exertions of that able viewer, Mr John Watson of Willington, for being the first in this neighbourhood to patronise an invention pregnant with such great utility to coal mines of every description. No less a number than 40 horses we understand, will be dispensed with in the collieries of Coxlodge and Kenton.'

chain system was complex, inefficient and rather fragile and the wooden track further increased the friction. But his locomotive included a vital component which is still an integral part of the railway today.

William Chapman.

William Chapman was an ingenious and multi-talented engineer. Born in Whitby in 1749, he went to sea early and became a captain, gaining practical mechanical experience on the way. He gave up his sailing career to join his father and brothers on Tyneside, where they took on the lease of Byker Colliery and, in 1778, installed the first Boulton & Watt engine on Tyneside. His next investment was in leasing and sinking the Wallsend Colliery, but the difficulties turned out to be enormous and ruinously expensive – by 1782 he was bankrupt. However, he had already shown an aptitude for engineering and mechanics and redirected his career. The following year he went to Ireland with Matthew Boulton and would remain there until 1794. By the time he returned to Tyneside, he had championed the Dublin Canal, engineered the Kildare Canal, built for it the first oblique arch bridge and been involved in a number of other civil engineering projects.

Chapman came back to the North East to survey a proposed canal from the Solway Firth to Newcastle. It was not built, but the link from the Irish Sea to Newcastle would involve him for the rest of his life. Now accepted as a leading waterways engineer, he spent much of his career building everything from drainage schemes to docks to complete harbours. His base remained in the North East and here he rekindled his colliery interests. He was a partner in the

Kenton and Coxlodge, building for it the iron waggonway later converted for the Blenkinsop engines, although he had sold his interests just before, and he patented the first 'coal drop' where waggons could be lowered to the ships' holds for emptying, avoiding the breakage associated with the traditional spouts.

With his knowledge of mechanics, engineering and the coal trade, he was in a unique position to contribute to the development of the locomotive. Although his chain engine at Heaton did not progress, his 1812 patent had another feature. Chapman realised that using a number of axles could spread the weight of the engine and avoid problems with the track breaking. But then the wheelbase would be so long that it would have trouble turning on the bends – it would tend to derail or at least damage the track. His answer was to divide the wheel frames into one or two groups that could swivel independently – the 'bogie'.

This he used in his Heaton locomotive and in the same year, 1813, suggested that 'long carriages, properly constructed, and placed on two separate sets of wheels, eight in all, may take 30 or 40 people with their articles to market.' Both ideas were remarkably advanced pro-

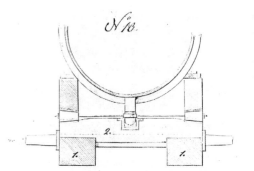

Chapman's bogie design, drawn in his own hand, 1813.

posals and even today the bogie remains a basic design element of long locomotives, waggons and carriages. But both were also very slow to catch on in Britain, where they were hardly used until the 1870s. In America they were appreciated much sooner, so much so that the bogie became perceived as its own invention.

Chapman's second engine was a refinement of his Heaton design. The Lambton Collieries near Chester-le-Street were owned by John George Lambton, later Lord Lambton, the famous 'Radical Jack'. He inherited his father's great estates when only five years old, so in his minority the pits were leased out under the control of a board. When he reached 21, in 1813, he took back direct working of the collieries and agreed with his advisors that a comprehensive update of the waggonway system was necessary. The following year, Lambton and his board decided to order an engine from William Chapman, regrade the lines and fit them with iron rails as a necessary step to making the system completely locomotive-run. The trial engine was built by Phineas Crowther who had an engineering shop on the Ouseburn near Heaton. Crowther invented the vertical winding engines that became such a feature of the pits in the North East (the last survivor is still steamed at Beamish Museum) and was a skilled and inventive mechanic, which was fortunate as the Lambton engine was a particularly complicated design.

The locomotive was tested on the waggonway at the very end of 1814. According to newspaper reports, it had eight wheels to spread the weight as in Chapman's Patent, and it worked by adhesion on the lesser gradients but where they grew too severe and wheelspin threatened, a chain had been laid that the engine could engage, as at Heaton. No detailed descriptions exist of this remarkable engine, but Crowther drew plans for another locomotive in 1814 and these have survived. They have no chain mechanism, but they do have eight wheels mounted on two separate frames, all of which were connected by gears. Both frames seem to form bogies,

> On Wednesday last, the 21st inst. a locomotive engine, built by Mr Phineas Crowther, was set to work on the waggon-way of John George Lambton, Esq. It drew after it eighteen loaded coal-waggons (weight about 54 tons) up a gentle ascent rising five sixteenths of an inch to a yard, and went nearly at the rate of four miles an hour. The engine was mounted upon eight wheels, according to a patent granted to Messrs Wm and Edw. Chapman, by means of which the weight is so far reduced upon each wheel, as to avoid the expence of relaying the ways with stronger rails.

Newcastle Courant, *24 December 1814.*

and while the amount of movement on them is not clear, here seems to be what would be classed today as an 0-4-4-0. When the complexities of that are added to the chain assistance device then here was a mechanically ingenious machine.

Chapman's locomotives had not been ordered for Heaton and Lambton by chance. The viewer of both these collieries was John Buddle, a local man born and raised near Kyo. He was the leading mining engineer of his day – popularly known as 'the King of the Coal Trade', a title he would maintain up to his death in 1843. Buddle Road at Benwell, a Wallsend street and its Industrial Estate and Arts Centre are named after him. He was immensely influential, an innovator, an enthusiast of mechanical power, a great tester of new techniques. He supported and publicised Chapman's patent locomotive; it was natural that they should be ordered for the collieries that he oversaw and where he could personally conduct the trials.

Buddle lived at Carrville, alongside the famous Wallsend Colliery which he managed as well as viewed. It is no surprise that the third Chapman locomotive

John Buddle

was tried here. The *Steam Elephant* (see page 43) demonstrated a change of design, simpler, with neither bogies nor any chain assistance. It had all of its six wheels connected to make the first 0-6-0 configuration, an arrangement that would be a favourite for short-range freight locomotives to the end of steam. The builder was Hawks and Co. of Gateshead; they supplied a kit of mechanical parts to the colliery to be assembled through the summer of 1815. Again the trials were disappointing; the wooden rails of the waggonway proved unsuitable. It was tried the next year at the sister colliery of Washington, but again failed, and was laid aside until Wallsend had converted its waggonway to iron.

WILLIAM BRUNTON

Quite the strangest of all the locomotive designs was run at Newbottle, near Houghton-le-Spring. In 1812 the colliery built a new iron waggonway from the pits to the harbour at Sunderland, so avoiding the need to trans-ship the coal by keels. It was a long, ambitious line that included a steep bank where extra horses, 'helpers-up' were needed, with running costs that were considered exorbitant. Owner, John Douthwaite Nesham agreed to try a locomotive designed by William Brunton, who was the chief engineer of the Butterley ironworks in Derbyshire where Chapman's Heaton

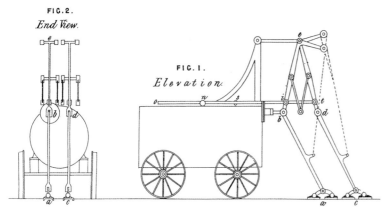

Brunton's legendary patent design of 1813.

engine had been built. In 1813 Brunton patented an engine arrangement for railways or canals which used steam-powered legs for propulsion. His 'horse to go by steam' was in the tradition of trying to mimic mechanically the actions of the natural world, just as the first attempts at aeroplanes were based on imitating the flapping of birds' wings.

This has long been viewed as laughable but, before locomotive design had an established set of rules, it was not as ridiculous as it seems. The trial engine Brunton built at Butterley seems to have had some success, or at least enough for Mr Nesham to test a larger version on his Newbottle waggonway. Quite what it looked like is unknown – it has been established that the patent design itself could not have worked – but essentially it was a boiler on wheels with probably two cylinders powering a pair of jointed legs at the back that 'walked' along the trackbed. Remarkably, Brunton claimed it worked through the winter of 1814, and was rebuilt in the following year, 'The facility with which it could be regulated in slipping upon, or over anything was very perfect. I was permitted to enlarge the new boiler because … the tendency of the engine in operation was to raise the engine off the rails.' But disaster was only weeks away.

For the Newbottle Colliery, 1815 was to be a year of misfortune. The Wear keelman, recognising that the waggonway was a threat to their livelihood, burnt down the Sunderland staiths. In June there was a massive blast at the colliery killing 57 people. The grand unveiling of the improved locomotive at the end of July was to be a celebration, a new beginning. Near Philadelphia, a large crowd assembled round the engine with nine year-old pit-boy John Holmes, the first miner to be rescued from the ruins of the pit, given pride of place by the boiler. To make the demonstration as effective as possible, steam was raised to the maximum pressure, then more as the driver strapped down the safety valve. The explosion was heard for miles.

The Newbottle Explosion

From *The Durham County Advertiser* 5 August 1815

'On Monday last, a melancholy accident occurred upon the waggon-way belonging to the owners of Newbottle Colliery. A new boiler having been procured and annexed to the travelling steam engine, used in drawing the loaden coal waggons up the ascent of the rail-way, it was tried for the first time on the above day, when the engineer, it is supposed, too anxious for its success, had overcharged the boiler with steam which caused it to burst with a tremendous explosion. Upward of 50 persons, men and children, we lament to say, have been wounded or scalded by the destructive accident. Three persons have already died, viz.:–Wm Sharp, the manager of the engine, who was blown a considerable distance, and most dreadfully mangled; Wm Nesbitt, one of the overmen of the colliery, and John Holmes, a pit-boy. Several others remain in a dangerous state. For the three persons who died immediately, the coroner, in ease of the parish, gave permissive warrants for interment, deferring his inquest until the result of the other sufferers, now lingering, should be known.'

It will never be known how many were killed. It seems that there were at least a dozen, including the unfortunate John Holmes, with many more injured. 'The top of the boiler weighing 9 cwt. was blown to a distance of 144 yards – Sharp, the engineer, was blown further than the boiler top – his body was most shockingly mutilated.' Philadelphia had seen the world's first great railway disaster – and the last of the 'steam horse'.

THE WYLAM ENGINES

It is taken for granted now that 'adhesion', the grip of smooth wheels on smooth rails, is effective, even though it appears to be in the face of common sense, but it is also limits the performance of the engine to a balance of gradient, rail condition, power and weight. This envelope seemed even more restricting in these pioneering days of locomotives when engines had to be light to prevent rail breakage, waggonway gradients could be locally severe and wooden rails were susceptible to slippage from wet and frost and there was no reason to think that iron rails would behave any differently. Horses had no problems in this regard; the Blenkinsop rack, the Brunton legs and Chapman's chain systems were understandable attempts to avoid the locomotive wheelspin that limits adhesion even today. As late as 1821, when Edward Pease of Darlington first saw Stephenson's adhesion locomotive, he '… was at a loss to conceive how the Engine could draw such a weight, without either having a rack with teeth laid in the ground and wheels with teeth to work into the same, or something like legs…'

At the Wylam Colliery west of Newcastle, a conscious effort was made to study the principles of adhesion. Together with his viewer, William Hedley, and foreman wright Timothy Hackworth, Christopher Blackett undertook a series of experiments in late 1812, using a test carriage loaded with iron blocks, driven along by men turning the wheels. This established that there was a direct relationship between the weight acting on a powered wheel and the amount of grip it had on the rail. The more weight, the more adhesion, a general rule that still applies to locomotive design today.

Hedley would later declare that he was ' … the person who established the principle of Locomotion by the friction or adhesion of the wheels upon the rails …' and the same important claim is often made for George Stephenson. Neither is true. Almost ten years before, Trevithick had relied on this same process for the Coalbrookdale, Penydarren and Gateshead engines, as well as the

THE TEST CARRIAGE AT WYLAM.

later *Catch Me Who Can*. The value of the Wylam trials was that they clarified the demands and limits of adhesion and these rules were then applied in practice to their colliery locomotives. They were the first adhesion engines to undertake regular economic work and so were highly significant, particularly as they demonstrated to an interested local market that rack, chain, leg or other systems might be unnecessary.

Their first engine, built by local engineer Thomas Waters, and based on the Gateshead Trevithick design, was mounted on the test carriage. Hackworth's son would later write that it '... showed strikingly the spasmodic, intermittent irregular action so characteristic of these early one-cylindered, fly and spur wheel-driven, cast iron boilered locomotives; often the auxiliary 'crow bar' was brought into requisition to move it off the dead points ...' These integral problems were added to by mechanical defects and a chronic shortage of steam. After a year that showed promise rather than outright success, Blackett agreed to three, more advanced, engines being built.

THOS. WATERS & CO.
MANUFACTURERS OF TREVETHICK ENGINES,
BEG Leave to return their Thanks to their Friends for the many Favours conferred upon them, and that they still continue to build the same Engines at their old Manufactory; and they further add, that they have succeeded in greatly improving and simplifying the said Engines, since they made them for the old Agent, John Whinfield, appointed in 1805, and since that Period they have been solely appointed by the Inventor to make them for Home Consumption or Exportation.
T. Waters & Co.'s Steam Engines have given great Satisfaction.
Gateshead, May 31, 1815.

Newcastle Courant, *3 June 1815.*

Two of these, *Puffing Billy* and *Wylam Dilly* (see page 46), would remain at work for some 50 years and become world famous (the third, *Lady Mary*, would be scrapped at the end of the 1820s). Their design followed Trevithick's in using a U-shaped or return flue to improve steam raising but was otherwise a quite different arrangement nor did it copy the Murray type. Instead it had two cylinders placed on either side of the boiler barrel rather than in its top, using parallel motion instead of slide bars. It was a perfectly good alternative but the first of the engines soon showed a fundamental problem. Wylam was unique amongst the major North Eastern collieries in using plate rails with unflanged wheels rather than the usual edge rail. In comparison they are weak and, with all the engine weight on four wheels, there was unacceptable breakage

---

Black Billy – the terrible devil

Samuel Smiles, writing in *Lives of the Engineers*, 1857.

'A story is still current at Wylam, of a stranger who was proceeding one dark evening down the High Street Road, as the 'Black Billy' (for so the locomotive was called) was seen advancing, puffing and snorting its painful and laborious way up from Newburn. The stranger had never heard of the new engine, and was almost frightened out of his senses at its approach. An uncouth monster it must have looked, coming flaming on in the dark, working its piston up and down like a huge arm, snorting out loud blasts of steam from either nostril, and throwing out smoke and fire as it panted along. No wonder that the stranger rushed terrified through the hedge, fled across the fields, and called out to the first person he met, that he had just encountered a '"terrible deevil on the High Street Road"'

of the plates. To spread the load there was a redesign which gave eight wheels on two frames, evidently with an amount of play built in, so essentially resembling the Chapman bogie – it is likely that he was responsible for the new arrangement.

The date of these engines is important for the effect they may have had on designs elsewhere, but it presents a problem. The first Trevithick-type locomotive was probably built early in 1813 with the improved twin-cylindered design ready either late in 1813 or early in 1814, and so after the Chapman and the Blenkinsop engines. The conversion to eight wheels took place towards the end of 1814, just the time when Chapman was completing his similar eight-wheeler for the Lambton waggonway.

The doubts on the dates are compounded by the conflicting claims later made by the families of Hedley and Hackworth. Each sought to diminish the reputation of the other whilst attempting to magnify their own role in railway history. William Hedley was born in 1779, the son of a grocer at Newburn on Tyne. He trained as a viewer, was appointed to Wylam but left in 1824 to pursue his own colliery and business interests. Timothy Hackworth was six years younger, born at Wylam where his father was foreman blacksmith. Timothy initially followed the same trade at the colliery, but would later be appointed resident engineer to the Stockton & Darlington

Railway (S&DR), followed by a distinguished career in locomotive building. It may never be known which of the two men was mainly responsible for the adhesion trials and the designs of the locomotives. What is clear is that Christopher Blackett's vital persistence and support is too often forgotten.

A Wylam 8-wheeler on plate rail, from Wood's 'Treatise' of 1825. All the wheels were gear-connected and it is likely that at least one of the two frames acted as a bogie, giving a design open to all sorts of problems – but it evidently worked.

GEORGE STEPHENSON'S LOCOMOTIVES

George Stephenson (see page 52 and following for a full account) was born in a cottage beside the Wylam waggonway. He had left the area well before any of the engine trials, but he must have been well aware of their progress and the success of adhesion as a working practice. His first locomotive was ready for testing in June 1814, so he had had the opportunity to see the Blenkinsop engine at Coxlodge and the Chapman engine at Heaton. From these he distilled his own design which was essentially a Blenkinsop-Murray locomotive without the rack system but dependant on adhesion instead. The engine worked reasonably well but lacked steam and its gearing proved jerky. The following year he took out a patent for an improved design which did away with the gears and directly drove the wheels, which were combined by a chain joining the front

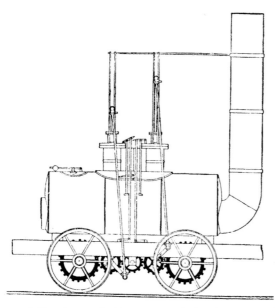

Stephenson's first design of 1814, gear-coupled and owing much to the Blenkinsop/Murray engine.

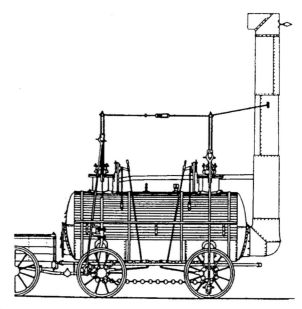

Stephenson's 1816 engine. The modifications show his increasing confidence as an engineer.

and rear axles. This simple but effective arrangement was to be the basis of his locomotives for the next ten years, although both the direct drive and chain coupling had been used before by others and the patent was probably invalid. This small problem had no effect on his career however; the reputation of George Stephenson was established.

Delays and cancellations

The short period of 1812-15 was very important; it had seen the first resurgence of locomotive development following the withdrawal of Trevithick. They had been successfully introduced at Middleton in Leeds and at the Orrell Colliery in Lancashire. But the greatest concentration was firmly placed in the North East. By the summer of 1815 there were engines in use at Kenton and Coxlodge, Heaton, Lambton, Newbottle, Wallsend, Wylam and Killingworth. The future of the steam locomotive would appear to be assured.

In fact it turned out to be highly premature. In May 1815, Coxlodge had a dispute with a neighbouring colliery that saw the Blenkinsop engines damaged and unusable. That same month, Heaton Colliery became flooded out and all production stopped – the Chapman chain locomotive was adapted to help pump out the seams. His complex design at Lambton was not in service as the new iron waggonway remained unfinished, nor was it to be a success when the line was completed. It has already been seen that the Wallsend engine proved unsuitable for the wooden track and how in July the Newbottle engine had suffered a disastrous explosion. By the end of the year the locomotive engine had proved itself only at Wylam and Killingworth. This dramatic period of design and experiment had turned out to be a false dawn – no similar burst of activity would be seen for another decade.

Although several of the engines had been withdrawn through accident rather than failure, the trials had shown that the locomotive still suffered some fundamental problems. It was not easy to produce a reliable high pressure engine. A design that worked when it was stationary did not necessarily translate to one that was moving – the stresses and strains on rough track racked the mechanism, the rails themselves were so light that the weight had to be kept to a minimum and this demanded such a small boiler that sustained steam production was always a problem. Rail breakage, expensive and disruptive, constantly bedevilled this pioneering period. There was a fine balance between the essential weight needed for an effective engine and the considerable added costs of stronger iron rails. Their conflicting demands would restrict the general adoption of the locomotive until the 1830s.

These trials had been made, not out of curiosity, but in pursuit of profit. The locomotive was only economic if it replaced the expense of horses but that made the movement of coal totally dependant on this new and unproven system. So it was a brave – or foolhardy – colliery that committed itself wholly to the locomotive in this state, nor had these local trials shown that it was always successful. Two more major events in 1815 slowed the progress of the engine. The battle of Waterloo ended the Napoleonic Wars with a lessening of the costs of horses, whilst a banking crisis reduced the confidence needed for major investments in experimental technology.

Despite these setbacks the region had learned valuable lessons – what worked and what didn't, that adhesion was likely to be a better prospect than racks, chains or legs and hence that waggonways must be more carefully graded and with gentle bends, that it was essential to improve the strength of the rails. And where the engines had been judged a failure they were often replaced, not by horses, but by self-acting inclines or cable haulage – the process of mechanisation had become unstoppable.

The locomotive entered 1816 battered but still breathing. Wylam quietly plugged on with its 'Billies' and 'Dillies', satisfied that they worked well enough so that no improvements were to be

Wylam Dilly *about 1880, preserved at Craghead. The long-running Hedley/Hackworth arrangement placed the cylinders alongside the boiler.*

made to them for over a decade. But Stephenson continued to experiment with his Killingworth designs, modifying, developing, testing. Here he was considerably helped by one of the Killingworth viewers, Nicholas Wood, whose better education meant that they formed a strong partnership of technical knowledge allied to practical, intuitive engineering. It has long been believed that work on the locomotive was being continued by these two alone between 1816 and 1825, but now it is known that the partnership of Buddle and Chapman continued their experiments at the same time. They had Phineas Crowther build an engine for the Whitehaven Colliery in 1816, bought back the Lambton engine and rebuilt it for a new Heaton waggonway in 1820, put the *Steam Elephant* back to work at Wallsend, this time successfully on iron rails, designed a locomotive for Rainton Colliery in 1822 and later developed a locomotive crane.

Their interests appear to have been purely to get a specific job

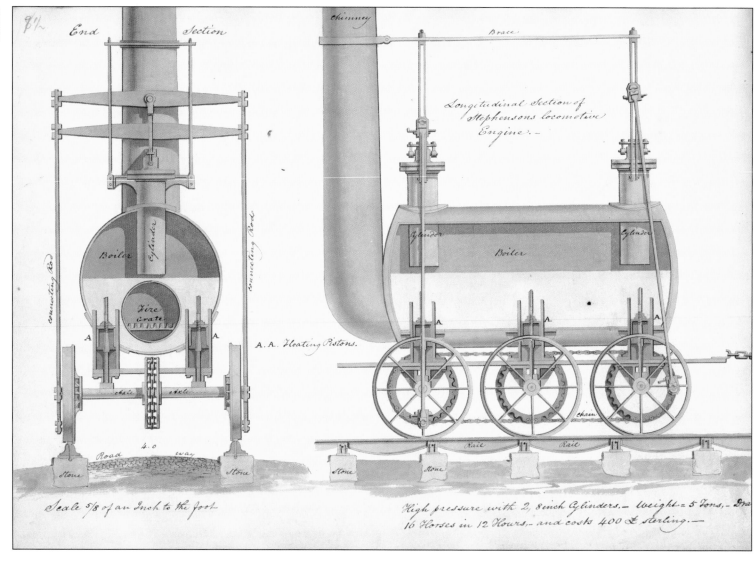

William Strickland prepared a version of Stephenson's 1816 Patent drawing for his important book Reports on Canals, Railways, Roads ..., *published in America in 1826. It shows, in 6-wheel form, the finished Killingworth-type engine, with direct drive to the wheels, chain coupling, steam springs and working on his lap-jointed cast-iron rail.*

done, be it transporting coal or moving stone blocks. Stephenson had a wider view of the powered railway – increasingly he was becoming the recognised consultant on new lines. He supplied a six-wheeler to the Kilmarnock & Troon Railway in 1816, the first locomotive in Scotland, and it is probable that another went to the Llansamlett waggonway in south Wales. But although he is now fundamentally associated with the locomotive, he recognised at the time that it was often a limited, almost specialised alternative to the incline or the stationary engine. When he built the famous Hetton railway, he was to use cable haulage for much of its length, although it was to be the locomotives that caught the public eye. His careful (and well publicised) development work on the Killingworth engines had come to the attention of some of the leading engineers of the day. With his appointment, first to the Stockton & Darlington, then the Liverpool & Manchester railways, he became the best known railway engineer in the country, the first choice for the great projects to come.

Wylam birth notices

Stephenson had been born just east of Wylam; it is remarkable that within just a couple of miles of this small Tyneside village came such important railway figures as Hedley, Hackworth, and Wood. A similar cluster is found around Pontop, birthplace of John Curr, inventor of the plate rail, John Steele of the Gateshead engine and that formidable innovator, John Buddle.

THE STEAM ELEPHANT

One of the most remarkable stories of the early locomotives to emerge in the last few years has been that of the *Steam Elephant*. In 1931, the Newcastle librarian and railway historian R.N. Appleby-Miller came across a map of the northern coalfield which was decorated with a picture of a very early six-wheeled engine. Its appearance caused a lot of interest as it did not seem to illustrate any of the known locomotives used in the region. Was it a sketch of one of Stephenson's first machines of 1814, or a Chapman design, or was it perhaps no more than an artist's whim and had never existed at all?

The first sighting of the **Steam Elephant**, *decorating a hand-drawn map of the Northern Coalfield.*

An exhibition in Newcastle in 1965 showed a large watercolour of the same engine, again from a local source but with the title *The Locomotive Engine or STEAM ELEPHANT*. The controversy was rekindled, but it did at least seem to be a real locomotive – the details were the same and it now had a name. An oil painting of the identical engine (reproduced on the back cover of this book) was tracked down in 1995 by Beamish Museum, who realised that not only was this was the earliest 'fine art' representation of any

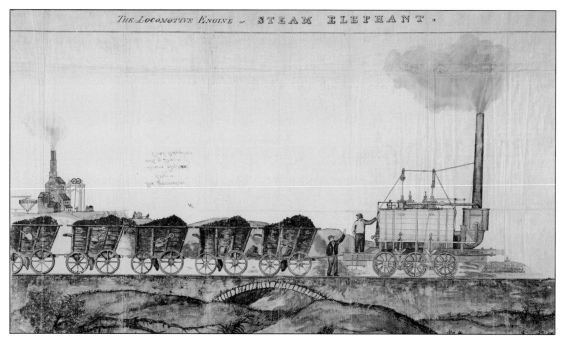

THE LOCOMOTIVE ENGINE or STEAM ELEPHANT.

The watercolour confirmed the name; Chapman and Buddle described most of their engines as 'Steam Elephants'.

locomotive, but if it had existed then the known history of the great engine trials in the North East must be at the least incomplete. The quest to identify the *Steam Elephant* would take two years.

The painting showed the *Elephant* in an identifiable landscape, with what had to be the Tyne on the right and the distinctive shape of Carville Hall in the middle distance, so the location was certainly North Eastern and appeared to indicate Wallsend. But the Heaton, Bigges Main, Kenton & Coxlodge and Wallsend collieries all had waggonways coming down to the staiths there. As its appearance didn't match either the Blenkinsops of Kenton or the Chapman engine at Heaton, and as the other two pits were not known to use locomotives, the location of the site did not automatically identify the engine.

The crucial evidence came from a fragment of an old account book. There was no title page, but it did have entries that detailed how Hawks & Co. of Gateshead had supplied the mechanical parts for a six-wheeled locomotive in the spring and early summer of 1815. A closer analysis of the accounts showed that the colliery concerned was clearly Wallsend. This was a real surprise, because although its pits were the most famous coal producers of their time, they had only short wooden waggonways and they had always been thought to be horse-hauled. Confirmation came with the well-timed purchase by Beamish of an important viewer's notebook compiled by Matthias Dunn, who recorded that, by the end of 1815, 'Wallsend … have started a Travelling Engine, but the wood ways obstruct it much', and would later tell how it was also tried at Washington Colliery.

Further papers were found that showed it returned to Wallsend and worked successfully on a new iron waggonway. The colliery connection also meant that the engine must have been ordered by John Buddle, viewer and manager, and so was likely to have been designed by his associate, William Chapman, and this was confirmed by comparing the locomotive to that built by them for Whitehaven Colliery. After 66 years, the mysterious *Steam Elephant* had been identified.

Two more sketches were found, one of which not only showed that the *Elephant* was either modernised or had a sister engine but suggested that its base later became Hetton Colliery, the famous

The newly-completed replica at Beamish in November 2001. Fitted with modern safety devices (such as brakes!) it worked superbly.

site of Stephenson's waggonway and engines. So the history of that railway, unquestioned for over a century, also had to be reconsidered. In fact the results of this hunt for the *Elephant* led to a general reassessment of the story of the North Eastern pioneers, this new information on previously unknown engines, makers and locations suggesting that there may yet more to find.

There was one more twist to the story. Beamish had built a recreation of an early nineteenth-century waggonway on which the replica of *Locomotion* gave rides to the public. The Museum decided to build a full-size working *Steam Elephant* to accompany it and work began on the very difficult task of translating the side view of the watercolour and oil paintings into a set of three-dimensional engineering drawings. The engine was successfully completed at the end of 2001 and opened to the public the following March. Not only is it the first standard-gauge steam locomotive to be built this century, but the use of the *Elephant* on the Pockerley waggonway must surely make this the shortest 'trunk' route in the world.

Puffing Billy and Wylam Dilly

The three short years between 1812 and 1815 were fundamental in demonstrating that the locomotive could be effective, in discovering what could or could not work, in pointing to the way development needed to go. It is remarkable that two engines remain from the period and even more so that they should both be from the same small Tyne colliery of Wylam. They are the oldest surviving locomotives in the world, the earliest representatives we have of a system that would change the face of the world. But they also symbolise, with *Locomotion* and *Rocket*, the tremendous imaginative energy that flooded the North East early in the nineteenth century, that made it a byword for innovation and technical excellence.

To appreciate *Puffing Billy* and *Wylam Dilly* today needs a leap of imagination. When they were built there were perhaps 25 miles of locomotive-powered railway; by the time they were retired there were tens of thousands of miles, a staple of the western economies,

Hair's charming view of Wylam Colliery. In 1835, one of the engines was noted as having travelled 17,000 miles and hauled 64,000 tons of coal in the past year.

perhaps the greatest advance in land transport since the invention of the wheel. The engines themselves are small, battered and crude; it seems hard to see how they could drag more than their own weight, yet they would combine a hundred years of hard work pulling coal trains. From 1814 until the early 1830s, they powered the only railway that was purely locomotive-hauled. As the first economic adhesion locomotives, these primitive-looking machines were the direct ancestors of the railway engines of today.

They looked even less elegant in their early lives. First built with four wheels, these had to be doubled to prevent breakage of the plate rails, so until the end of the 1820s they had a very distinctive appearance, with all eight unflanged wheels driven by gears (see page 39). When the waggonway was converted to stronger edge rail, they were rebuilt with a slightly different motion and on four wheels to give their present appearance. They were possibly originally called after two of Blackett's daughters, *Elizabeth* and *Jane*. *Puffing Billy* is a nickname, perhaps after the asthma suffered by 'Billy' Hedley, as is *Wylam Dilly*, which is the local dialect for a small carriage.

Billy went to the Patents Museum (now the National Museum of Science and Industry) in 1862. Wylam owner Captain Blackett, an irascible and extremely difficult man, then spent three years trying to get the museum to buy what was a completely worn out relic for enough money to replace it with a more modern engine. That the museum eventually agreed a more reasonable price of £200 is fortunate.

Dilly went off on her own adventures in 1822. During the keelmen's strike, all movement of coal upriver from Newcastle was stopped. In an attempt to break it, the Wylam Colliery bought a keel and had Hawthorn & Co. engine it with *Dilly*, converting it into a small paddle tug which, complete with military protection, towed the keels downriver. The fireman at the time was John Lawson – he carved his initials on the boiler and they are still there

Old Locomotive Engine
Wylam Coll.

Tho. H. Hair.

One of the Wylam locomotives, painted by Thomas Hair about 1840. The Trevithick-type boiler means that the driver is at the opposite end from the fireman, which cannot have helped visibility. In 1860, the colliery viewer reported that a man had fallen asleep on the line, '... it was quite dark and the Engineman not seeing him, he was cut to pieces ...'

*In 1906, the Royal workshops in Munich built an exact working replica of **Puffing Billy**, now on display in the Deutsches Museum.*

today. He later became a driver on another railway where he was known as 'Hell Fire Jack' because of his reckless speeding. He was eventually dismissed, sank into alcoholism and drowned near the inappropriately named 'Comical Corner' at South Shields. His engine was more fortunate. When Wylam closed and was sold off in 1869, the old locomotive fetched the princely sum of £16 10s – its scrap price. But it was bought by William Hedley's sons as a memorial to their father and so preserved, restored and then proudly displayed at their Craghead Colliery. It was loaned to the Royal Scottish Museum in Edinburgh in 1882 and can be seen there today.

The distinctive design of the Wylam engines was not followed by any other locomotive builder except one. John Urpeth Rastrick was born in Morpeth in 1780 – his unusual middle name came from his mother and it originates from the hamlet next to Beamish. Rastrick was apprenticed to a Shropshire iron works, where he

probably worked on the first locomotive of all at neighbouring Coalbrookdale. He certainly built Trevithick's London engine of 1808, *Catch Me Who Can*.

He was in the North East keeping abreast of locomotive designs in 1823 and 1825. When he was given an order for three engines for the Delaware & Hudson Rail Road in 1828, he based their general arrangement on the Wylam engines, with the cylinders mounted on the sides of the boilers and with a similar motion, but driving directly onto the wheels. One of these, *Stourbridge Lion*, was to be the first commercial locomotive to be tried in the USA – some parts of it survive in the Smithsonian Institution in Washington. Another of similar design, built for the Shutt End Railway in the West Midlands, the *Agenoria*, is on display in York's National Railway Museum.

The Light from the North

There remained one fundamental problem that frustrated the general adoption of the steam-powered railway. The fragility of the rails had bedevilled the development of the locomotive from its first days; constant breakages were not only expensive but disrupted the working of the line whilst the resultant need for engines to be as light as possible stunted their performance and practicality. The L-shaped plate rail, so popular in Wales and much of the rest of Britain, quickly proved unsuited for locomotive use – its design meant that it was fundamentally weak and dirt trapped in the rail corner led to added friction. The edge rail used in the North East proved to be better, but still the use of cast iron resulted in it being both brittle and expensive. It was also only available in short lengths, and as a result there were a multitude of joints that led to track unevenness and greater stress on the locomotives. Until a better solution could be found, the development of the locomotive was bottlenecked.

It was realised that the answer might lie in using wrought rather than cast iron; stronger, more pliable, cheaper and with the potential to be rolled into long lengths of line. It had its own problems of production and design – their solution was to be one of the great breakthroughs of railway history and once again it was to take place in the North East.

In 1819 the manager (and later partner) of the Bedlington Ironworks near Blyth was Michael Longridge. Although Sunderland born, his family had a long association with both these works and with Hawks & Co. of Gateshead, so he was familiar with the practicalities of metallurgy and of railways. When the neighbouring Willow Bridge Colliery approached him to build a waggonway to the works, he made himself aware of the experiments that had been tried with wrought or 'malleable' iron and determined to develop a suitable rail. The new design is credited to the Bedlington agent, John Birkinshaw, who came up with a wedge-shaped rail which was light and strong but still retained a large bearing surface. Not only that, but it could be rolled into lengths of 18 feet or more, rather than the typical three or four feet of cast rails. Birkinshaw patented the design in 1820, its abilities were proven on the new colliery line and quickly

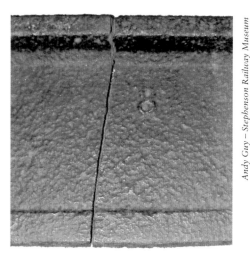

The granular appearance of a (cracked) cast iron rail, above, contrasted with the stringy grain of the slimmer malleable rail.

appreciated by railway engineers.

Stephenson wrote in 1821 that the new rails '… are so much liked in this neighbourhood that I think in a short time they will do away with the cast iron railway …' and insisted on their use for the new Stockton & Darlington Railway. The great Scottish civil engineer, Robert Stevenson, considered the new line the best of its type that he had seen. The promoter, William James, who inspired the Liverpool & Manchester Railway, wrote that same year that '… light has at length shone from the North and I pronounce it as my candid opinion that the malleable iron railroad at Bedlington Works is by far the best I have ever seen, both in respect of its material and form …' A deputation from the Railway later inspected and approved of the rail.

The arguments over cast versus malleable iron were to rumble on for some years, but once the early quality problems were solved there was no contest. The rails were to develop into a number of designs over the years but the 'Age of the Railway' was to be firmly founded on the rolled malleable rail. Its strength, lightness and length allowed the development of heavier and more powerful locomotives – it was not superseded until the general adoption of steel some forty years later. It was as significant a breakthrough for trackwork as the famous Rainhill Trials were to be for the locomotive; Birkinshaw and Longridge deserve more fame in their native region.

By the early 1820s the technology was in place to allow what is now thought of as the 'modern' railway: powered; built for a variety of loads and run by a public company established for that reason. The first was famously the Stockton & Darlington Railway (S&DR), with its initial engine, *Locomotion*, a variation of the Stephenson Killingworth Colliery designs, which could themselves be traced back to Murray. The engine was significant as the first locomotive to be built by Robert Stephenson & Co. of Forth Banks in Newcastle. Robert and his father, George, were partners in the

Andy Guy – Darlington Railway Museum

Locomotion, *preserved at Darlington. Its status as an icon was recognised as early as 1846, when it headed the opening train of the new Redcar line – perhaps the first celebration of railway history.*

company, together with Edward Pease of Darlington, his cousin Thomas Richardson and Michael Longridge of Bedlington. Its great impact was that, at the time, it was the only engineering firm that was willing and able to build locomotives 'on demand'. Although the Murray designs still ran at Leeds and Wigan, their design was already obsolete; Hedley was content to run his engines at Wylam alone; whilst Buddle and Chapman, although still experimenting, restricted their locomotives to collieries under Buddle's control. In effect, Robert Stephenson's was the only locomotive-building company in the world.

The Stockton & Darlington was, in fact, something of a half-way house between the old colliery waggonway and the complete modern railway. Although planned for mixed freight, its core business was the movement of coal from the pits of south west Durham to the port of Stockton. In this it was very effective, opening up a production area previously cramped by the limits of road transport and at the same time halving the price of coal at Stockton within just eighteen months. However, much of this was moved by horse power rather than by locomotives and by contractors instead of by the railway company itself. It did have passenger traffic, but that was unexpected and this too was moved by horses until 1833.

But it did demonstrate that long railways could be built for profit, as a business in themselves rather than a branch of a production process such as a colliery, and that passenger traffic could be a significant added bonus to the freight traffic. This was consolidated by the publication in 1825, the same year that the S&DR opened, of Nicholas Wood's *Practical Treatise on Rail-Roads*. Born near Wylam, Wood had been George Stephenson's closest collaborator in the trials of the safety lamp and the Killingworth locomotives. He would later have a distinguished career as a colliery viewer and mine owner; he supervised the building of the Newcastle & Carlisle Railway, engineered the Brandling Junction Railway in north Durham and was a director of the Newcastle & Berwick. His

*Stephenson's homage to his home area: the **Northumbrian** engine was driven by George himself at the opening of the Liverpool & Manchester Railway.*

Treatise became the accepted manual on the planning and building of the new powered railways, expanded in 1831 and 1838 with further editions published in America and France.

The accomplishment of the S&DR and the influence of Wood's *Treatise* established in the public mind the success of the 'Newcastle' mode of railway. Edge rails not plate, of wrought iron not cast; the beginnings of a 'standard gauge' based on the 4ft 8ins used at Killingworth, Hetton and Darlington; the increasing dominance of the locomotive, with its unrivalled potential for further development in contrast to the restrictions of horses and cable haulage. All were confirmed by the adoption of these features by the Liverpool & Manchester Railway, locomotive-hauled, company-run, a full inter-city service built with passengers in mind. The modern railway had truly arrived – the western world would race to Tyneside to get their own built.

George Stephenson – Father of the Railways?

George Stephenson is popularly known as the 'Father of the Railways'. The great writer of technical histories, L.T.C. Rolt went as far as to suggest that he might be 'the most famous engineer who ever lived'. The story of his rise from a humble, uneducated colliery mechanic to the heights of the mechanical engineering profession was at the core of Samuel Smiles' best selling *Lives of the Engineers*. The very embodiment of the virtues of 'self-help', George Stephenson has become a moral lesson as well as an heroic success.

The bones of this spectacular rise are certainly true. He was born in 1781, the second son of Robert Stephenson, a colliery engineman at the Wylam pits. His birthplace still exists, alongside the route of the old waggonway, but its appearance is deceptive. The Stephenson family did not have sole use of this pleasant country cottage. The whole family, eight in all, occupied just one room.

George Stephenson's birthplace at Wylam, with the path of the waggonway on the left.

As was the way, George followed the trade of his father, and quickly proved an unusually able engineman. By the age of 22 he had married, had a new-born son, Robert, and a good job running the ballast engine at Willington, with a cottage supplied. For a man of his origins, his career was already a success. The following year, 1804, he was promoted to the responsible job of brakesman at the large Killingworth Colliery, just to the north of Newcastle and he moved to the village.

His personal life then suffered a tragic setback. First, his newly born daughter died, followed shortly after by his wife, Mabel. For a short time he escaped to Scotland where he worked a mill engine, then returned to Killingworth and his old job at the pit. But his

George Stephenson, from Samuel Smiles' Lives of the Engineers.

Dial Cottage, Killingworth. George and Robert lived here in the formative years between 1805 and 1823.

ambitions went much further than that. His great talent was a natural understanding of mechanics and this he demonstrated by fixing a new engine at the colliery that no one else could make work. George had a gift for seizing an opportunity and here it paid off very well – when the colliery enginewright was killed shortly after, George replaced him and took on further responsibilities for the owner's pits elsewhere. He was, at 31, a made man.

The following year, 1813, he started work on a locomotive for the Killingworth waggonway, supported by the 'Grand Allies', the powerful syndicate that owned the colliery. This first engine, *My Lord*, was completed in July 1814 and proved promising, probably joined by another, *Blucher*, later in the year. At the beginning of 1815, with the Killingworth viewer, he took out a patent for improvements to the design, replacing the cumbersome gear train

with a chain to combine the two axles.

His reputation began to spread and when he developed a miner's safety lamp later that year, the resultant publicity brought him to the attention of the wider technical community. Controversially, it was claimed that Stephenson's lamp had been invented before that of one of the leading scientists of the day, Sir Humphry Davy, and a fierce argument ensued. Was it really feasible that an uneducated mechanic had made one of the greatest ever improvements to mining practice? Or was it quite unfair to deny him the credit just because of his background? The facts are still disputed, but a general consensus is that both men developed lamps at the same time, but independently.

In 1816 he patented more improvements to his locomotive and for the next four years not only experimented further but developed a wide-ranging consultancy on waggonways and mine engines. He had made the leap from clever mechanic to leading local engineer, with enough prosperity to take a share of a coal mine himself. But it was in 1821 that he seized two great opportunities which would make him a leading national name. The first, in partnership with his elder brother Robert, was for the provision of mine engines and the construction of a waggonway for the major new colliery being sunk at Hetton. The principal promoter was Arthur Mowbray,

---

HETTON COLLIERY IN THE COUNTY OF DURHAM.
This day is published, price **7s. 6d.** elegantly printed upon a sheet of drawing paper,

A PERSPECTIVE VIEW OF THE WORKS OF THE COLLIERY, the Horizontal, Inclined, and Self-Acting Planes, with the Loco-Motive and other Engines used on the Railway, and the Straiths, and Self-Discharging Depôt on the Banks of the River Wear, near Sunderland; with a SECTION of the PIT and STRATA.

London: Sold by Thomas Sotheran, No. 2, Little Tower-street; and Baldwin, Cradock and Joy, Paternoster-row.

Interest in the Hetton Colliery justified the production of prints for a wide distribution.

who had been impressed by George's advice on earlier projects and who now gave the two brothers the difficult task of building a line over severe hills direct to the port at Sunderland. When it was completed in 1822, the combination of stationary engines, self-acting inclines and three brand new Stephenson locomotives formed a wholly mechanically powered railway which generated great interest nationwide.

The second – and career making – breakthrough was George's appointment to re-survey and engineer the Stockton & Darlington Railway. No mere colliery waggonway, this was a major railway of over 25 miles, opening out the south west Durham coalfield and joining two major towns. It was a public line, owned by the share holders and expecting a mixed goods traffic. At his first meeting, George greatly impressed the principal promoter, Edward Pease. When he later took the usually dour Quaker businessman to see his Killingworth engines, Pease was hugely excited by the possibilities of using locomotives rather than horse traction. He persuaded his banker cousin, Thomas Richardson, to join with him in a partnership with George and George's son, Robert, to establish an engine factory in Newcastle – Robert Stephenson & Company – and a railway engineering consultancy to be known as George Stephenson & Son.

The opening of the S&DR in 1825 was a triumph for George. With a procession led by the factory's first locomotive (now known as *Locomotion No. 1*), the load capability and stamina demonstrated by this engine was the first great public showing of the possibili-ties of the modern, steam-powered public railway. It caused something of a sensation – Stephenson had been projected into the national, and international, spotlight as interest in railway building grew into the first 'mania' of speculation.

Even before the completion of the S&DR, Stephenson had been appointed to oversee other rail projects. The most important of these was the proposed Liverpool to Manchester line, the first great scheme to join two major cities. The line was difficult, with major engineering works necessary, but by 1829 the main problem remaining was the choice of how to power it. George was strongly in favour of using locomotives, but the Darlington railway, which still relied on horses for much of its work, had not yet convinced some senior engineers of its usefulness compared to the known performance of stationary engines and cable haulage. A competition was agreed on to test the most modern locomotive designs – the Rainhill Trials – and this was convincingly won by Stephenson's new engine, *Rocket*. The railway opened the following year with a stable of *Rocket*-type locomotives and, despite the tragic fatal injury of MP William Huskisson on the inaugural day, it was a spectacular success. The complete modern railway, public, steam-powered, had arrived and with it the basic design of locomotives for the next 130 years.

George's son, Robert, had played no small part in this triumph. His father had insisted on the best available education for him, even when money had been short. An apprenticeship as a colliery engineer at Killingworth proved short-lived due to his delicate health,

The triumphal opening train of the Stockton & Darlington Railway, 1825.

but Robert gained practical experience assisting in the survey for the Darlington and Liverpool railways and was made the managing partner of the Newcastle factory established in his name. In 1824 he took an appointment to manage mines in South America and was away for three years. On his return he not only took control of the Robert Stephenson works but engineered three lines himself.

George and Robert, the established expert and the rising star, dominated much of the railway boom of the 1830s and 40s, with contracts that included the Grand Junction Railway and the London & Birmingham, the first of the great trunk routes that were to create a national rail network. But George was already starting to wind down his workload. He had made a fortune, not just from his railway work, but by exploiting mineral deposits found during construction in Derbyshire. The acknowledged figurehead of this great new railway age, he enjoyed honours from home and abroad (including the first Presidency of the new Institution of Mechanical Engineers) – as well as the challenge of growing straight cucumbers. He died in 1848 at his fine house near Chesterfield and was

Robert Stephenson, from Smiles' Lives of the Engineers. *Unlike his father, Robert was patient, sociable and unprejudiced, with a good relationship with his colleagues.*

Newcastle, 1862. The unveiling of the George Stephenson monument brought one of the largest crowds ever seen in the town.

buried in the local church under a simple stone.

Robert's career proved famously successful. With his friends and competitors, Joseph Locke and Isambard Kingdom Brunel, he fundamentally changed the country and its infrastructure. His tubular bridges at Conway and Menai and his High Level across the Tyne were masterpieces of nineteenth century engineering, but one of his greatest satisfactions was the completion of the East Coast main line through Newcastle and Northumberland. Always rather delicate in health, he died, worn out from overwork, just eleven years after his father and was buried in Westminster Abbey.

George Stephenson's rise from pit mechanic to world famous engineer is often thus presented as inevitable, untroubled and heroic. It was not at all so straightforward. More than once the 'Father of the Railway' came close to being no more than a footnote of history.

His early rise to enginewright at Killingworth had been a measure of his raw ability, hard work and unremitting ambition. He was fortunate in that he could observe the trials of the existing local engines: of the Blenkinsop rack engine at Coxlodge; the Chapman chain locomotive for Heaton Colliery; and the adhesion experiments of Hedley and Hackworth in his native Wylam. His first engine, on which he may have been advised by John Buddle and William Chapman, turned out to be neither revolutionary nor particularly original in design. Instead he had taken the best parts of two successful designs, the engine arrangement of Murray and the adhesion of Wylam, to produce what was effectively a Blenkinsop engine with the rack removed and driving instead on all four wheels. It was simple, practical and reasonably effective and became the basis for his engines for the next dozen years.

His patent improvement the next year, 1815, introduced a chain to connect the driven axles rather than the previous cumbersome gearing. This too worked well, although there is strong evidence that it was not his invention at all but had been suggested by others some time before. In 1816, a further patent covered improved rails and the use of 'steam springs' on the engine to lessen the damage done to them. These were the main design elements of his famous Killingworth engines – a Murray-type general arrangement together with his own chain coupling and steam springs – and it was to prove the most effective of all the pioneering locomotives of the time.

His engines owed much to others, but three factors made him the outstanding locomotive engineer of that period. First, he was not content with engines that just worked, but continually strove to improve them, making minor changes and adjustments, carefully testing the results, trying yet again. In this methodical work he was greatly helped by one of the young underviewers at Killingworth, Nicholas Wood, an educated man with engineering training and a more socially respectable background. Wood was invaluable in

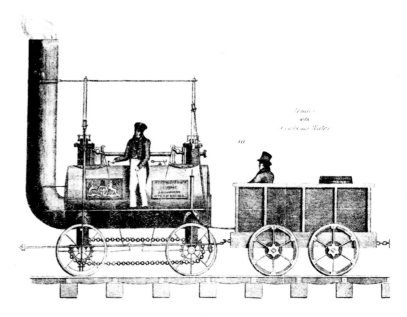

Stephenson's Patent Engine. It is significant that this print was used in Birkinshaw's promotion of the malleable rail, a fundamental improvement supported by Stephenson against his own cast iron design.

analysing, presenting and publicising the results of these engine tests to the influential figures in the colliery and engineering professions, in a way that the socially awkward and barely literate Stephenson could not have done.

Secondly, George was allowed by his Killingworth employers to work elsewhere. He was given the career space to act as a mechanical consultant and hence to promote his designs beyond the colliery. The other pioneers, such as Chapman, Buddle, Hedley and Hackworth, concentrated on solving the specific waggonway problems of their own colliery interests, rather than promoting them on the general market. Blenkinsop had been active in selling his designs elsewhere, but by 1816 it was becoming clear that his rack system was a development dead end and neither he nor Murray seemed to have worked further on other solutions. Following the disappointments of the 1815 trials in the region, it seemed that Stephenson alone was prepared to make locomotives for other interested parties. Those he sold to Scotland and South Wales were not successful, but his Hetton engines made a considerable impression in a market that was his alone.

Finally, he appreciated that locomotives were not an end in themselves but part of the railway system. Many other engines had 'worked', but had proved of limited practicality when their weight and stresses broke the rails. It was a problem that had bedevilled the take up of the locomotive from the time of Trevithick's first engines and was not to be solved until the development of the malleable rail in the early 1820s. Stephenson spent much time improving cast iron rails, and when the new rails came out he immediately pressed for their use on the S&DR. Until then he recognised the fact that locomotives were often not the best choice for the waggonways he was consulted on, but that frequently, as at Hetton, stationary engines and inclined planes were better suited. By his appreciation of these realities he built a reputation as a sensible and experienced waggonway consultant. In addition, as a general engine builder and designer, he could offer himself as a complete railway engineer, able to survey, construct and provide the power for new lines, be it for stationary or for locomotive engines. As a result, when interest in new railways restarted in the early 1820s, he had established a strong reputation as a leading specialist in the field.

His enthusiasm for steam captivated Edward Pease and Thomas Richardson. They realised the commercial potential of the new powered railways and hence the possible market value of George Stephenson. Determined to make the most of their find, they not only backed the Robert Stephenson factory and George Stephenson consultancy, but purposely set about 'remaking' their man to maximise their investment. In what could be seen as a remarkably modern marketing exercise, they raised his modest fees to those of the country's leading engineers, on the basis that people expect to pay the best prices for the best advice. They arranged to spread the word in the investment markets for the rash of new rail-

Andy Guy – Stephenson Railway Museum

It flatters to deceive. This Doulton tile picture vividly illustrates Stephenson showing Edward Pease his Killingworth locomotive. Unfortunately, the engine is actually **Puffing Billy** *from Wylam.*

way projects that only a Stephenson line would make money and hence make a killing on the chosen shares. And they decided that the image of the man himself would need to be improved. He was too rough a diamond and needed polishing so that he had some of the manners and appearance of a top professional engineer rather than a local mechanic made good. He was instructed in his dress (including the essentials of clean underwear) and removed from the distracting company of his unsuitable friends.

This had some effect, but it was too much to expect that George would totally submit his career and his personality to their control. Following his Hetton and S&DR appointments he was the man of the moment in this first 'mania' of railway building. Too hungry in his ambition to refuse work, other contracts led him to spend too little time completing the Darlington railway. It ran late and hugely over budget in his absence. Nor did he give enough of his time to the firm of Robert Stephenson's, which was floundering and near closure while Robert himself was in South America. The locomotive patents that were expected of George to protect his market lead and promised work for the factory were not forthcoming.

In all, Pease and Richardson were in some despair of the monster they had helped to create, and even the source of much of his distraction, the Liverpool & Manchester project, was nearing disaster. George had spread himself too thinly there as well, leaving much of the survey work to his team of young and inexperienced apprentices. When its railway bill was discussed in parliamentary committee, the powerful canal lobby had a field day with George, demonstrating the many grave errors and incompetencies that were liberally scattered through the survey. He was humiliated and the bill was thrown out. Together with the crises at Darlington and Newcastle it looked very possible that George Stephenson's star had already burned out.

His career was saved as much by the support of others as by his own abilities. Pease and Richardson shored up the finances of the Newcastle works until Robert's return injected a new dynamism and inventiveness. Pease loaned sufficient funds to the S&DR for it to be completed – its subsequent success restored much of George's reputation. As a result, the directors of the L&MR were confident enough to re-employ their disgraced engineer and here too he was able to reap the credit when the line opened.

He was re-established as the leading figure of the 'railway revolution', reaping further contracts and great rewards both at home and abroad. But within a few years, the market was becoming aware that George was perhaps better as a name to have attached to their project than as an active engineer in its construction. In what was becoming a scientific age, and with railways that were growing more complex and expensive, his characteristic gifts of intuition rather than analysis, the sometimes error-strewn nature of his surveys and his rather informal control of construction contracts was becoming increasingly unsuitable. His own locomotive designs progressed little beyond the 1820s, his model remained that of his sturdy colliery workhorses – slow, reliable, of limited but proven performance. But the engine market now was snappy, competitive, fast changing – looking for continued dramatic improvements in speed and performance. After Robert's return in 1827, George had limited impact on the engines that came from their factory and, after the early 1830s, played almost no part in them.

Despite these practical shortcomings, he remained the great symbol of the railway movement, the new stars Brunel, Locke, Gooch and his own son, Robert, notwithstanding. His reputation would be cemented by Samuel Smiles' biography, fixing firmly in the minds of generations the story of the 'Father of the Railway' (a term used in his own lifetime), rising from his humble roots to be the hero of the transport revolution that had, in a few short years, transformed Britain, Europe and North America.

So what was Stephenson's significance? He didn't invent the railway and he didn't invent the locomotive. He did not invent two of the staple design features of the modern steam engine – the blast pipe and the tubular boiler – although they are often credited to him. His own locomotives were frequently based on the work of others and were ultimately mired down in conservatism – he pro-

Locomotion, *photographed in 1916 against an added backdrop. Like* **Billy** *in Newcastle,* **Locomotion** *was for years displayed at Darlington Bank Top station, giving ECML passengers no escape from the promotion of the North East as the 'Cradle of the Railway'.*

duced no major patents after 1816. His part in the design of *Locomotion* is uncertain, whilst its successors the ground-breaking *Rocket* and *Planet* classes are the work of Robert and his Newcastle staff. The Hetton waggonway had to be redesigned only a few years after completion, the S&DR suffered from faults in construction and delays due to his absence. The L&MR was compromised due to his mistakes and inattention. Embarrassing errors in his work on

the Grand Junction Railway led to his replacement by his old apprentice, Joseph Locke. His name is attached to the great London & Birmingham Railway, but it was clearly understood at the time that Robert must be the engineer in charge and his father's role limited to the survey and to friendly advice. For most of the major projects of the 1830s and 40s, the Stephenson expected to bring them to fruition was Robert, not George. It might even be

An Italian bronze plaque presented for the Centenary of the Stockton & Darlington Railway. The anniversary celebrations of 1875, 1925 and 1975 have been regarded as the world focus for railway history and George Stephenson its prime character. Stephenson engines were to be the pioneering locomotives in the USA, Canada, Russia, Belgium, Germany, France, Austria and Italy – although they owed more to Robert than to George.

said that only luck and the support of his friends had saved him from the disasters of 1825. Had they not, his characteristics of determination, ambition and confidence might instead have been judged as a fatal combination of arrogance, incompetence and bad judgement.

But they were not. George Stephenson remains the outstanding figure in the development of the modern railway. His early engines may have been somewhat unoriginal but they were sensible and practical, the work of an experienced and intuitive mechanic who was evolving into an engineer capable of improving his designs with ingenuity, thought and careful experimentation. He thought through the effective uses of steam power on the railways, in their arrangement and in the essential need for better rails. His personal charisma is reflected in the support given to him throughout his career – by the Grand Allies and Nicholas Wood at Killingworth, Arthur Mowbray at Hetton, Pease and Richardson, the board of the L&MR. And he was fortunate in his timing. He had little competition as the first dedicated railway engineer, but having put himself in that position, he grasped the opportunities that followed with confidence and determination. He was difficult to work over and under, and almost impossible to work with. He was bombastic, never wrong, a man who boasted of his modesty but overlooked the support of those who had helped him. But he was also loved and respected. In the end, and on a grand scale, he proved to be right in much that he had done and lucky in how it had gone. Ultimately, these are the primary requisites of a great man.

A Head of Steam – the Spread of Tyneside Railways

The popular perception of Newcastle's place in the railway system is as part of the East Coast Main Line. However, that took a long time to happen – the town was the final and quite late link in the London-Edinburgh trunk route. Before that, it was served by a number of other railways, one of which has its own claim to fame.

Britain's first coast-to-coast railway, and the first public line to serve the town, was the Newcastle & Carlisle Railway (N&CR). It had a long and difficult birth, first conceived in 1794 as a canal linking the North and Irish Seas and starting from Lemington. A second proposal the following year suggested a beginning from a wet dock close to the Ouseburn Bridge and bending to the north of Percy Street and Gallowgate. Then followed a succession of alternative and often bitterly argued proposals, principally centred on whether the route should go to the north or south of the Tyne. Despite getting as far as a Parliamentary committee hearing, the various supporters were ultimately so divided over the route that nothing was done except survey after survey. The construction costs were certainly formidable, the returns on the money arguable and there were practical problems with the locks needed to breast the Pennines and the water supply that would be necessary.

In 1800 a very different solution was put forward. William Thomas of Denton Hall, a successful land agent, recommended an iron plateway between Newcastle and Carlisle. With this system, ordinary road carriages and carts of the right gauge could access the way at any level crossing to make an early roll-on, roll-off railway. The scheme got no further.

The opening in 1823 of the short canal from Carlisle to the Solway Firth stimulated proposals for a connection to the Tyne once again. This time, however, a normal edge railway was recommended, starting from near the Close at Newcastle and with a projected cost less than a third than that of a canal. In 1825 the principle was accepted and the Newcastle & Carlisle Railroad Company formed, with shares quickly taken up.

Again it fell foul of squabbling about the route. The first proposal to Parliament suggested a course mainly on the south side of the Tyne, with a terminus near the Tyne Bridge, on the quayside, and a branch from Elswick Dene to Thornton Street to serve the west end of the city. George Stephenson then suggested an alterna-

Iron Ways

From Louis de Gallois: *Des Chemins de Fer en Angleterre, notament a Newcastle*. In *Annales des Mines* (vol 2, 1818) translated by Sheila Bye.

'… Iron ways can be established on a much larger scale. They seem destined to take the place of canals … they are already occupied on a project of this nature to join, by Newcastle and Carlisle, the east and west coasts in the north of England; and no doubt, if that project is carried out … that in a few years these roads of iron will traverse Great Britain in every way …'

A ridiculous idea!

From *The Tyne Mercury,* 16 November 1824
'What person would ever think of paying anything to be conveyed from Hexham to Newcastle in something like a coal-waggon, upon a dreary waggon-way, and to be dragged for the greater part of the distance by a roaring steam engine? The thing is too ridiculous to dwell upon …'

tive route north of the Tyne and coming down to the Ouseburn via the Town Moor. Further proposals, objections and detours led to the postponement of the bill until 1828, when it was again presented as starting from the quayside and including the Elswick branch. Arguments continued about the interests of the landed gentry and the course of the line, but the very poor existing communications between Newcastle and Carlisle, together with the proven success of the Stockton & Darlington Railway, now made it unstoppable. The Bill was finally passed in May 1829, at 63 miles the longest railway approved by Parliament so far, but with locomotives specifically forbidden.

Despite further arguments about the route, construction started the following year and the first portion, Blaydon to Hexham, opened at the end of 1834, with the use of locomotives agreed shortly after. There was still debate about what route it should take to serve the towns of Newcastle and Gateshead, further complicated by other proposed railways that wanted to enter the towns. After lengthy negotiations the line was extended to Redheugh in 1837, with passengers and goods taken across the Tyne by boat to the Newcastle quayside. So the town gained its first 'station' – no more than a wharf close to the company offices at 66 The Close.

This could be only a temporary solution, for the town and the railway. Within two years, the Newcastle & Carlisle had bridged the Tyne at Scotswood and opened a station in Railway Street. In that same year, 1839, the Newcastle & North Shields Railway (N&NSR) built a temporary terminus near Manors and the Brandling Junction Railway opened Oakwellgate Station in Gateshead.

THE WRONG SORT OF RAIN –
The opening of the Newcastle & Carlisle Railway
On 18 June 1838, the opening of the line from Redheugh to Carlisle took place. But what should have been a grand event quickly became a great farce. When the invited guests were getting on one of the steamers at the Newcastle quay, a gangway collapsed, dumping a dozen or so into the river in all their finery. After a prolonged

A detail from J.W. Carmichael's view from Redheugh, where the Newcastle & Carlisle united with the Brandling Junction Railway. Passengers were brought by steam boat from Newcastle.

Caught short

From a pamphlet by William Martin ('Christian Philosopher'), *Mismanagement of the Railway Directors on the Opening of the Newcastle & Carlisle Railway, June 18, 1838.*

'... As far as I could judge, it appears that the railway men were making sport upon people when returning from Carlisle. They would sometimes stop the train; and it was natural to suppose that some would wish to go out for necessary purposes. Then, in a minute, the whistle was heard; and, for fear of being left behind, the gentlemen came running away without taking time to adjust their dress. It was pitiful, but one could not help smiling; and I cannot think what condition the ladies were to be in, as some of them had been sitting for several hours ...'

breakfast, the civic dignitaries were taken to the train but found that the crowds had invaded the reserved carriages 'and the chief magistrates of Carlisle and Newcastle were obliged to look for refuge in a pig cart' whilst others had to get what seats they could in open carriages.

Finally, by 12.30 and now very late, the procession of thirteen trains set off on the 61 mile trip, with one engine fitted, perhaps uniquely, with a steam organ at the front. Not only were there delays *en route*, but it rained solidly all the way to Brampton. By the time the last train came into Carlisle, at 6pm, it was already an hour past the time it should have set off back to Newcastle. After a stampede for refreshments the arranged procession through town had to be cancelled and there then followed an undignified rush for the few remaining seats for the return journey. While the engines

OPENING
OF THE
NEWCASTLE AND CARLISLE
RAILWAY,
On the 18th Instant.

NOTICE IS HEREBY GIVEN,

THAT

The MAIN Procession of Trains to CARLISLE,
Will leave the Redheugh Station at 11 o'Clock in the Morning.

No Person can be allowed to enter the Station, or be admitted to the Trains, without a Ticket, on any Pretence whatever; and the Entrances to the Station, both by Land and Water, will be closed at 15 Minutes *before* 11 o'Clock precisely, (in order to allow Time for the necessary Arrangements) after which Time no Person can be admitted.

The Trains will proceed to the *Canal Basin*, CARLISLE, where Parties may leave to obtain Refreshments in the Town. But the Trains, on their *Return to Newcastle*, will depart from the *London Road Station*, Carlisle, at 5 o'Clock precisely.

* * No Person can be allowed to go upon the Engines or Tender.

Newcastle and Carlisle Railway Office,
June 11th, 1838.

were turned and the line checked, passengers were kept waiting in the open for some three hours, many of them in light summer clothing. The rain continued.

On the way back, one train hit the back of another, with two passengers injured and causing a further long delay. The first passengers did not get back to Newcastle until 3am, the last not until six in the morning, nearly eighteen hours after they had set out. It was, in every way, a memorable day.

AND EAST TO THE COAST

The line to North Shields was given Parliamentary approval in 1836 and opened three years later. That was remarkable progress, for although the line was only seven miles long, it needed dramatic engineering works. It began by Pilgrim Street, crossed Trafalgar Street on a fine stone bridge followed by an embankment over Pandon Dene, but the two most spectacular features were the viaducts over the Ouseburn Valley and Willington Dene. Both were designed by the father and son team of John and Benjamin Green, local architects, who had already built a number of notable bridges. For these two crossings they used the unusual construction of stone piers supporting timber arches made of laminated wood, a successful technique that lasted until 1869, when they were replaced by a very similar design but in iron.

The Greens again used laminated timber for the arches of North Shields Station, which may have been the first use of curved ribs to support a station roof. In 1845 the N&NSR was taken over by George Hudson's Newcastle & Berwick Railway. Hudson

Tyne & Wear Museums

The viaduct over the Ouseburn Valley, in an engraving after J.W. Carmichael, 1838. The timber arches were replaced in iron, as seen on page 149.

NEWCASTLE AND NORTH SHIELDS RAILWAY.

THIS RAILWAY will be OPENED on the 18th Inst., with a Procession by the Directors, the Shareholders, and their Friends. A Train will leave the Station, Newcastle, at Half-past 11; and another at 1 o'Clock. There will be a Dejenner at Tynemouth at Half-past 2 o'Clock. On their Return, a Train will leave the Station at North Shields at Halfpast 5; and another at 7 o'Clock.

The Shareholders may procure their Tickets by applying at the Office in Pilgrim Street, after Friday the 14th Inst.

A Footway leads from the Office to the Station.

PERMANENT OPENING OF THE RAILWAY.

The Public is respectfully informed that it will be permanently opened on Saturday the 22nd Instant, for the regular Conveyance of Passengers and Goods.

PASSENGERS' FARES.

	s.	d.
Mail Carriage, ...	1	6
First Class Do., ...	1	0
Second Class Do., ...	0	6

Children under 10 Years of Age, at Half-price.

The Trains will run every Hour, (except during divine Service on Sunday Mornings and Afternoons) and call at the Walker, Carville, and Howden Stations. Further Particulars will be given in future Advertisements.

Railway Office, Pilgrim Street, Newcastle,
June 12, 1839.

retained the services of Benjamin Green and the following year used him to build a new eastern terminus for the line at Tynemouth, a handsome Jacobean design which has fortunately survived despite being superseded by later stations.

The railway was, however, having doubts about its Newcastle terminus. There were possibilities of connecting with other lines,

The original terminus of the Newcastle & North Shields at Carliol Square, c.1910, when it had long been reduced to a coal yard.

particularly the Newcastle & Carlisle, and of building a shared through-station. Rather than the commitment of the Pilgrim Street terminus, they compromised with temporary platforms and a rudimentary shed just to the east, later to become the coal depot known as Carliol Square.

GATESHEAD AND TO THE SOUTH

While the Newcastle stations for the Carlisle and North Shields railways were only short term solutions, Gateshead had by then a proper terminus at Oakwellgate. The Brandling Junction Railway (BJR) was instigated by brothers John and Robert Brandling to serve their extensive coal royalties in North East Durham. The route went from Gateshead through Felling and Pelaw to Boldon Colliery, where one branch went to coal staiths at South Shields and another down to Monkwearmouth. The first part to open was a stationary engine-worked incline joining Gateshead with the southern terminus of the Newcastle & Carlisle at Redheugh, allow-

ing that railway access to the staiths above the Tyne Bridge at Oakwellgate. The original intention had been for the Brandling to cross Gateshead in a tunnel. Instead, it was taken over the High Street on a viaduct, meaning that the station had now to be raised on a great earth mound in the grounds of the old Rectory, with an inclined plane taking the coal waggons down to the quay.

By September 1839, the Brandling line was open between Oakwellgate, South Shields and Monkwearmouth. Three years later it began a rudimentary passenger service on its branch to Tanfield and Marley Hill, via the Redheugh Incline, but for many the BJR had a reputation of being slow, dirty, uncomfortable and with primitive facilities. Where the Shields and Monkwearmouth lines branched near Boldon, a connection was made with the Stanhope and Tyne Railway, an ambitious and initially unsuccessful line that crossed the county to the Pennines before dropping down to Stanhope in Weardale. On its way, near Washington, it was joined to the Durham Junction Railway, a short line of only a few miles but which served the rich coalfield of central Durham. By 1840 there was a southern rail link, via the three companies, from

Thomas Hair's view of the Redheugh Incline c.1840, showing the stationary engine house, left.

BRANDLING JUNCTION RAILWAY.

THE DIRECTORS beg leave respectfully to inform the Public, that the Line of Railway from SOUTH SHIELDS to MONKWEARMOUTH, IS NOW OPENED, and that the Times of Starting from the Stations will be as follow,—commencing on WEDNESDAY, 19th inst.

From Sou Shields.	From Monkwearmouth.
1/4 past 8 Morning	1/2 past 7 Morning.
3/4 — 9 ,,	9 ,,
1/4 — 11 ,,	1/2 past 10 ,,
3/4 — 1 Afternoon.	1 Afternoon.
1/4 — 3 ,,	1/2 past 2 ,,
3/4 — 4 ,,	4 ,,
1/4 — 6 ,,	1/2 past 5 ,,
3/4 — 7 ,,	7 ,,

THE FARES ARE—
First Class Carriages, 1s. | Second Class, 9d.
Children under 12 Years of Age, Half-price.
N.B. The Gates at the respective Stations will be closed 5 Minutes before the Times of Starting.
Brandling Junction Railway Office,
Gateshead, June 18, 1839.

The landsale coal staiths at the north end of Oakwellgate mound. They will be integrated into Gateshead's new Sage centre for music.

near Rainton to Gateshead and it was this route that would play a major role in a much grander strategic plan.

In 1841 the Great North of England Railway opened a line from York to Darlington, with the intention of continuing to Newcastle and eventually Edinburgh, so forming a route down to London. However it ran out of money and a number of other companies were founded in the hope of completing the route to the Tyne. The interested parties met in Newcastle at the end of April 1841 under the chairmanship of George Hudson, agreeing a route from Darlington to Rainton, linking with the existing Durham Junction, Stanhope & Tyne and Brandling Railways, so continuing the line to Gateshead and with connections to South Shields and Sunderland. The new part of the route was to be built by a company called the Newcastle & Darlington Junction Railway (N&DJR)

which, under the control of Hudson, received its Parliamentary act in 1842 and started construction work the following year.

The trio of companies that the route plugged into were, at the same time, going through financial crisis. The Stanhope & Tyne effectively went bankrupt, to be reconstituted into two new companies, one of which, the Pontop & South Shields, took over the eastern part of the line and with it the link to the Brandling Railway, which was itself under pressure. Meanwhile the Durham Junction

SUPERIOR TRAVELLING
FROM THE TURF HOTEL AND QUEEN'S HEAD,
NEWCASTLE-UPON-TYNE,
AND THE KING'S HEAD INN, DARLINGTON,
IN DIRECT CONNECTION WITH THE GREAT NORTH OF ENGLAND AND OTHER RAILWAYS.
COACHES LEAVE NEWCASTLE FOR DARLINGTON.

1 March 1843, Newcastle coaching inn the Turf Hotel, advertises its services. Until the route to Gateshead was completed, coaches took passengers to the railhead at Darlington.

company was quietly going under and, in 1843, was taken over by Hudson's N&DJR. These links in the northern route were patched up financially, the new line completed to the south and, in May 1844 a ceremonial train opened the railway from York to Gateshead.

A month later, the whole route from London (Euston) to Gateshead was publicly opened, the special first train taking just over eight hours to run the 303 miles. It was a major achievement to knit together this strategic line using the routes of several competing companies, marked by a celebration in the Assembly Rooms in Newcastle which included a speech by George Stephenson on his own rise to fame from his Tyneside colliery beginnings. But when the route settled into regular work it became clear that trying to use a combination of lines owned by different companies was troublesome in the extreme. As a result, Hudson effectively strong-armed

NEWCASTLE-UPON-TYNE AND DARLINGTON JUNCTION RAILWAY STATION AT GATESHEAD.

the Brandling Railway into selling out to his N&DJR. It took over the line on 1 September 1844; on that same day the Brandling's terminus of Oakwellgate was closed to passengers with its role taken over by a major new station at Gateshead.

Hudson placed his new building in Greene's Field, alongside the Redheugh Incline connecting the N&C with the Brandling and N&DJ railways. It was designed by York architect, George Townsend Andrews, on a grand plan, a long single storey classical frontage for the booking offices and waiting rooms with a two storey refreshment area and small hotel. Well fitted out and enclosed with a two span roof, it was elegant and ambitious; Hudson's intention was to build alongside a high level road bridge across the Tyne to give access to Newcastle with the rail link to Berwick via a bridge downriver at Bill Quay. Newcastle was in danger of being sidetracked; there was a very real threat to the town's expectations of being the site for the major Tyneside station.

Andy Guy

Above: The long-derelict hotel is to be restored in the redevelopment of the Greenesfield site.

Left: Hudson's monumental Greenesfield Station, with the hotel to the left, from the Newcastle Journal, 22 June 1844.

The High Level Bridge and the Central Station

At the start of 1845, the need for a decision on a rail bridge across the Tyne and the demand for a proper station to serve Newcastle were becoming critical. By that time the Carlisle and the North Shields railways had, for several years, suffered their separate termini to be little more than temporary sheds whilst a joint building was discussed. South of the river, the Newcastle & Darlington Junction, the main route to the south, had opened its very impressive new terminus at Greenesfield. It now seemed likely that that the principal Tyneside station would be permanently located at Gateshead.

Newcastle town council was determined not to be sidetracked in this way. It controlled a large area of mainly unbuilt land in the Spital and Forth parts of town, on the south western edge of the grand developments by Richard Grainger. Here was a site of generous size, convenient for the newly fashionable centre, which could both serve and complement the town, away from the ancient, inconvenient and low-lying riverside area. Both the Newcastle & Carlisle and the Newcastle & North Shields railways could join here, the levels were not difficult, but it would mean that if a Tyne rail bridge was on an adjacent site it would have to be at 'high level' as well. The town also had a desperate need for a new road crossing – the old Tyne Bridge was inadequate and, with its steep approach banks, difficult to use and poorly placed for the new growth of the town away from the river.

Meanwhile, the planned Newcastle to Berwick line would need to join with Gateshead's southern route in order to give a connection from Edinburgh to London. But that did not mean it had to be built near the planned Newcastle station. Serious consideration was given to rail crossings near Scotswood or downstream near Bill Quay, both of which were potentially cheaper to build. But it was time that something was decided and, as usual, it was a compromise between political expediency and economic viability, seasoned with a dash of personal drive.

A print of 1840, proposing a bridge to connect the Brandling with the Newcastle & North Shields Railway.

Of the several proposals for bridging the Tyne, the Newcastle Town Council initially favoured the one suggested by John and Benjamin Green. This was for a high level bridge similar to the design they had used for the Ouseburn and Willington viaducts, adjacent to the station site, but it was only to carry a roadway. It had behind it the financial muscle of the 'Railway King', George Hudson, and he now became the driving force for the Tyne crossing. Still the need remained for a railway bridge across the river and one which could serve a major station for Newcastle.

Hudson's grand ambition was to continue his railway interests north to Berwick, and the most economical way to do that appeared to be to build a railway bridge on the narrow Bill Quay river crossing and to retain his new Greenesfield Station in Gateshead as the main station for the two towns, serving Newcastle with the proposed road bridge. But naturally neither Newcastle council nor the Newcastle & Carlisle Railway wanted this and Hudson needed the support of both for his Berwick railway. As a result he agreed, in January 1845, that a joint station would be built on the land offered at Spital, but proposed that the new bridge would be for the railway, together with space for a footway rather than a road. Further pressure from the council persuaded him to agree to building a combined road and rail bridge, abandoning the Greens' design but using the same site.

At last the main parameters had been settled. The station would be on the generous plot at Forth and Spital serving five railways: the Carlisle; North Shields; Brandling; Darlington Junction; and the new Berwick line. As for the crossing, it would be at a high level combining road and rail and set out just upstream from the old Tyne Bridge, bypassing the Quayside and the new Greenesfield Station, confirming the importance of the new Grainger area of town and downgrading Gateshead as a major transport hub. It was a major strategic decision, not just for the railways but for the future development of the two towns.

Hudson consolidated his railway strengths during 1845. He already controlled the route south to York and beyond. To the north, he absorbed the Newcastle & North Shields into his new Berwick railway, so that by 1847 he would have the main east coast trunk line consolidated into the York, Newcastle & Berwick Railway. But still his grand design was incomplete until the Tyne crossing was opened and here he was under some pressure – he had guaranteed it would be ready for traffic by the summer of 1850.

Hudson's promise of an early completion had been necessary but ambitious. At the time he gave it, in 1845, not only was there no design for the bridge itself, there was no

This view from c.1860 shows how completely Stephenson's bridge dominated the riverscape until the building of the present Tyne Bridge in 1928.

precedent for such scale and complexity. He was fortunate that he had two great local engineers to call on – Robert Stephenson and Thomas Elliot Harrison, both thoroughly experienced in railways and bridge building.

Stephenson was Engineer-in-Chief on the Berwick line, but was grievously overstretched at the time. Much of his workload was taken by Harrison, who had already engineered the Durham Junction line and built the great Victoria railway bridge over the Wear. The two men were old associates with a good working relationship; their combination of bold design with sound engineering would be the key to the success of the project.

It was a formidable problem. So as not to impede river traffic, they were allowed no more than four piers in the water, so the spans between them would be long. To meet the rails south of the Tyne, the track would have to be over 100 feet above the river; it had to combine road and rail traffic with approaches on the river sides to match. Money was limited, and so was time.

Their solution perfectly fitted these conflicting demands. If the bridge had road and rail alongside each other it would be so wide as to be ruinously expensive, and with level crossings needed at both ends, cause danger and delay. But if they placed the rail track above the roadway, the heights were convenient, traffic safely separated and the bridge a manageable width. The council was in favour of it being built completely in stone, but that again would be expensive and it was feared that its massive weight would be too

Andy Guy

much for the riverbed foundations. Masonry piers supporting iron spans – lighter, cheaper, faster to build – were the solution.

The exact design process of the bridge is not clear, as records have not survived, but the division of work was defined by Harrison in 1846, when he wrote, 'The plans have been prepared under my direction; the designs are not mine but my friend Mr Robert Stephenson's.' Their final specification gave three river piers of a height 140 feet from bedrock to the top, with piers and arches on each side to tie it to the land. Because the foundation strength was found to be weak, the river piers were made hollow to save on weight and cost.

The structure of the six iron spans was more involved. Each was nearly 125 feet long and had to carry rail lines above a roadway. Stephenson had, some years before, built a rail bridge over the Regents Park Canal with a 50 feet span. It was the first to use a deck suspended from a cast iron arch and this was an ideal tried and tested design for the Tyne – it needed little more than scaling up. It made allowance for the two problems of using iron in long structures. Cast iron is immensely strong in compression but weak in tension, and its brittleness can lead to it failing with little warning. Wrought iron is much stronger in tension and had greater flexibility but was expensive and, in plate form, only available in relatively small sizes.

Stephenson exploited these characteristics in his choices for the spans. The main loading was designed to be carried by the arches. As these were in compression, they could be made of cast iron. To stop them spreading, the tension was taken by wrought iron bars between the piers. The road deck was suspended by wrought iron rods from the rail deck above and in turn this double weight was taken by cast iron columns sitting on the arch and from there down through the stone piers.

Preparations had already been made for the masonry that had to be brought in, stored, shaped and transported around the site. This was a formidable task – each pier alone needed 5,000 tons of stone despite their 'lightweight' design and the total weight of masonry for the bridge and approaches was over 50,000 tons.

Although work progressed very well on land, it was a different matter for the river piers, the foundations of which had to be prepared below water level. A double ring of timber was driven into the river bed and puddle clay put between them to make a watertight coffer-dam. In the now-protected centre, nearly 12 feet of the river bed sand was taken out and iron-tipped bearing piles driven deep down to 'rock bottom' in one of the first uses of Nasmyth's steam piledriver. However the ground proved very difficult, the sand becoming so compressed at high tide that driving the piles often became impossible until the river level dropped again.

Some months late, the stone foundations were laid for the piers and now work proceeded briskly to build them up to full height. Only when this was done could the spans be fitted.

The contract for preparing and erecting the ironwork was awarded to Hawks, Crawshay & Sons of Gateshead, not only one of the leading firms, but very handily located just a few hundred yards along the riverbank from the site of the bridge. By July 1847 the first span was test-erected at Hawks' works and satisfactorily loaded to 800 tons, well in excess of its planned workload and one

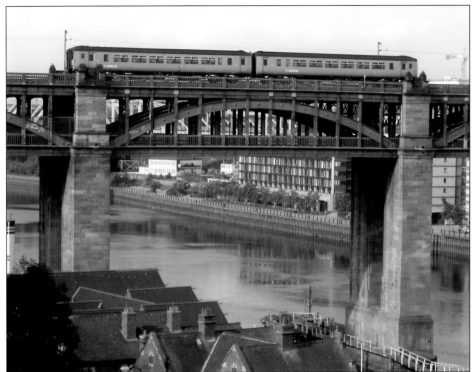

Andy Guy

The core design of the bridge, repeated six times across the Tyne and its banks.

of the reasons that the Bridge is capable of taking weights today that are far greater than any foreseen in the 1840s.

To erect the ironwork, Hawks had substantially to strengthen the wooden staging and cranes used for the masonry work and extend them right across the river – in effect, they built a railway bridge to build a railway bridge. The arch segments were taken on rails at roadway height, to be lifted into position by overhead cranes running on very wide tracks fitted above pier height, all supported by heavy scaffolding. In nine months all the main ironwork was completed and in August 1849 the first trial train was sent across. No problems were found, the Board of Trade Inspector

He erected a similar viaduct next to the uncompleted Border Bridge at Berwick so that by the middle of October the whole route was open from London to Edinburgh, with Newcastle firmly established as a hub in one of the great national railway routes. George Hudson, however, was about to fall from grace (see page 87).

(see page 87)

The official ceremony for the bridge took place on 28 September 1849. The train carrying Queen Victoria and Prince Albert stopped at a great temporary platform built alongside the central span, where the

OPENING OF THE HIGH LEVEL RAILWAY BRIDGE, AT NEWCASTLE-UPON-TYNE.

Great crowds watched the opening of the temporary viaduct on 29 August 1848. The crossing must have been a hair-raising experience.

approved the construction and the High Level Bridge was ready to open to railway traffic.

In fact, trains had already been carrying passengers over the river for nearly a year. The building of Hudson's Newcastle & Berwick Railway had been going on very well while the High Level was suffering its delays. So as not to have his great north/south route blocked at the Tyne, Hudson had the bridge scaffolding extended on the east side to make a temporary wooden viaduct and on this he ran trains across the river from the end of August 1848.

royal visitors were welcomed at a floral arch by the assembled worthies of Newcastle and Gateshead, with a crowd estimated at over 60,000 watching from the banks. Just over four months later the road carriageway was completed and the bridge completely opened. The total cost was £243,000, some £20 million in modern terms and eighteen per cent over the original estimate. For 57 years it carried all the rail traffic of the East Coast Main Line and for nearly 80 years it was the only high level crossing for road and foot passengers into the centre of town. As such it was the single most

The High Level Bridge, still at work, still impressive, more than 150 years later.

THE BUILDING OF A GRAND CENTRAL STATION

There were two main considerations for the new Central Station. As it had to serve the east-west lines of the Carlisle and North Shields railways as well as the north-south route over the new bridge, the only way to align the rails was to form the train shed on a curve. And as it was placed on the edge of the grand new 'Grainger Town' development of the town centre, it was considered important that its design should both reflect its classical style and symbolise the ambitions of Newcastle itself. As a result it was to combine pioneering engineering with bold architecture to make the most impressive railway station yet seen in Britain.

It was built as a partnership between Hudson's Newcastle & Darlington Junction Railway and the independent Newcastle & Carlisle, which had, for years now, been desperate to finalise its town terminus. Once the companies had reached agreement at the beginning of 1845, the N&C quickly got on with

important element of the Tyneside transport system and remains a significant link even today. The combination of road and rail on one bridge is still an unusual formation, despite its great practical advantages. That it could combine adventurous engineering with such happy design makes it, as the official Grade 1 listing for the bridge says, 'one of the finest pieces of architectural ironwork in the world.'

building the viaduct needed between its temporary terminus in Railway Street and the joint site at Forth. The new line and its station opened to traffic in March 1847; this terminus, the third in the company's short history, was again only intended to be a short term measure, although delays in constructing the main building meant it had to be in use for nearly four years. The partner companies were soon joined by the newly formed Newcastle & Berwick Railway, and all three agreed on John Dobson as the architect of the station buildings, with the track layout in the hands of Robert Stephenson and T.E. Harrison.

The land had been mainly open space and had been set aside by the town council for some years as part of a restructuring of the

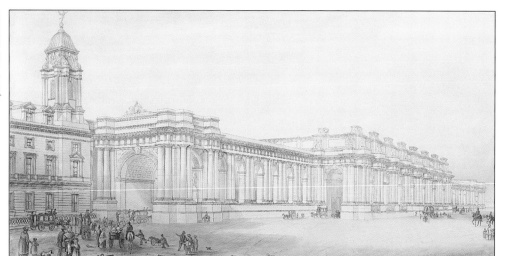

Above: Dobson's sketch of his original design for Central Station, and, below, Central as built, without the carriage drives and with a much reduced portico.

western edge of town, with consideration given to access for the N&C's terminus at Railway Street. It was a generously sized site and convenient for the new centre of town; it was indicative of the importance the council attached to a proper railway station for

Newcastle that they encouraged Hudson and the N&C directors to build here and build well. Dobson was the obvious choice, his grand designs had already transformed the New Town which the station site adjoined.

His plans for this new set-piece building were suitably ambitious. The Neville Street facade was heavily classical in style, featuring a massive central porte-cochère flanked by a pair of covered carriage drives, giving a great row of columns, tall arches and coffered ceilings. Its west end was a block of offices to serve as the headquarters of the N&C; their trains terminated at the platforms behind, whilst the east end was arranged for the working departments and refreshment rooms of Hudson's York to Berwick line and was later adapted as the head office for that railway as well. The drawings were approved by both railway boards in the summer of 1846 but various problems delayed the start of construction for over a year then led to its suspension for several months. Disaster was to befall Hudson himself – the great supporter for the grand plan disappeared. Money was now tight for his railway and his successors imposed economies that meant that the carriage drives would never be constructed and his massive porte-cochère would be built only in a simplified form in 1863, after pressure from the town council. This resulted in several changes to the frontage, with a reduction to a relatively modest Italianate facade, to the great disappointment to both the architect and the town. If Central Station seems imposing today, then how grand a scheme it would have been if the original design had been built as planned.

The train shed and interior underwent some small changes but they were substantially as originally designed by Dobson. The triumph was his shed roof, where he used not just three spans of some 60 feet each, but curved them to follow the line of tracks to form a

The station interior in a sketch by John Dobson. Looking east, it shows the magnificent airy sweep of his train shed.

shed of great majesty and engineering ingenuity. To take the load, Dobson used a system not dissimilar to that of the High Level Bridge, with wrought iron tie bars transferring the stresses of the roof to the side walls and columns – he had already used a timber version in his Grainger Market interior of 1835. To allow the curve,

he used, for the first time in Britain, wrought iron ribs, which were themselves curved to support the arched roof and which required a new technique developed by Hawks' engineering foreman. The final effect was to give the station an interior that was as ambitious as the facade but which added the drama of the great high spans,

Queen Victoria and Prince Albert arrive at Central Station on 29 August 1850. Their trip to Scotland officially opened the East Coast route to Edinburgh. The Keep, seen through one of the railway arches, is still a classic railway view today.

end of August 1850, the station was ceremonially opened by Queen Victoria and Prince Albert, commemorated by the sculpture of their heads over the entrance to the main concourse. Central Station, despite the architectural compromises forced onto Dobson, was acclaimed a great success and one of the marvels of the railway age. The principal design elements of his roof were to be used in the great stations at Paddington, York and elsewhere; it pioneered the concept of the train shed as a great public space rather than just a practical working area, and was unusual for a major railway station as being the work of a single hand, when more usually the architect planned the buildings and an engineer the shed.

From the care by which it was placed and the generosity of its site, it was able to serve the east coast main line, be the terminus of the Carlisle, North Shields, South Shields and Sunderland routes and act as the headquarters of both the Newcastle &

arching and curving away in the distance. It remains spectacular today, but how much more so 150 years ago when, not only were such huge covered spaces hardly known outside cathedrals, but the interior itself was far less cluttered with footbridges and platform buildings.

The construction of the shed began in September 1849. At the

Carlisle and the York, Newcastle & Berwick railway companies, making Newcastle one of the very few great towns in Britain to have just one principal station. It remains today one of the finest buildings in the country – the region that had developed the modern railway had a fitting monument at last.

THE VIADUCT

There was one more essential element in the arrangements for the bridge and station. The level of the line over the bridge, and hence at Central Station, had been fixed at that of the Brandling Railway approaches. We have seen how the N&C had to build a viaduct to give access to the station from the west. For the line out to the east, shared by the Berwick and the North Shields railways, a more dramatic structure was necessary, bridging the great cuts of Dean Street and Manor Chare to join with the existing line near Manors. This was ideal for Newcastle – running so high, there would be no need for disruptive level crossings anywhere near the town centre, but it was an expensive decision for the railway company.

The parliamentary act that allowed the High Level also gave powers to buy the necessary land and construct the Newcastle Viaduct. The ground was cleared by March 1847 and building work began, using stone from Benton. The multi-centred Dean Street Arch is the most spectacular part, 80 feet above the road with a span of 78 feet and is the only part of the viaduct to have a decorative frieze. To cross St Nicholas Street, a handsome arched iron bridge was built by the Gateshead firm of Abbot & Co (see frontispiece painting by Thomas Hair).

Above, an early nineteenth century view after Thomas Allom of The Side, and below, dominated by the great arch of the viaduct.

Although the bridge, station and viaduct today remain fundamentally as built, they have had to adapt to 150 years of changing transport demands. The High Level Bridge appears the least altered but has also come the closest to wholesale destruction. In June 1866 a corn mill alongside the Newcastle end of the bridge caught fire and was soon out of control, with flames licking at the underside of the roadway. As this and the rail deck above were planked in wood and tar-coated, there was a very real risk that if the fire took hold, the whole bridge would burn like a torch and be completely destroyed. Frantic efforts were made to rip fire breaks in the roadway and get hoses to play on the areas alight; after several desperate hours the battle was won and the bridge saved. Repairs took some days, but the damage from the heat turned out not to be critical and the bridge reopened some days later.

The foundations had always been of concern and a careful check on them had to be maintained. When the Swing Bridge was constructed, the river was heavily dredged to allow the great battleships built by Armstrong's shipyard to come down the Tyne from Elswick and, although the height of the piers allowed ample clearance above water, the deepened river bed threatened their pilings. Just after World War I, in a complicated and delicate operation, the foundations were underpinned by concrete and given extra protection with coffer dams – there has been no great cause for concern since.

Train weights increased enormously over the working life of the bridge. When Stephenson first designed the structure, locomotives weighed only some 25 tons – 100 years later it had to deal with engines of over 150 tons, as well as vastly heavier carriages and waggons. It coped very well, but in 1890 it was felt necessary to strengthen the rail deck with steel box girders and add extra column supports. In the 1950s, the planking was replaced by steel troughs with the rails ballasted with stone chippings, a substantial extra weight for the spans to carry, which caused some concern.

The High Level Bridge under threat from fire in 1866.

Andy Guy

The damage from the fire can still be seen today on the north pier.

Central Station, looking west c.1860. Until 1984, iron barriers fenced off the platforms, forcing passengers to form long queues for many of the trains.

Although the structure seemed unaffected, the three tracks were later reduced to just two. The amount of rail traffic using the bridge had grown at a great rate through the nineteenth century and it was causing something of a bottleneck. By the turn of the century the bridge was taking almost 1,000 traffic movements a day and an alternative crossing had become imperative. The opening, in

Station changes

The layout of the interior of the station was changed quite considerably in the nineteenth century to deal with traffic changes. In its original form, the train shed had a far more open, even empty look than we are used to now. The platforms were only 15 inches above the rails and there were no buildings on them – the effect of this huge, almost flat space was quite different and must have been very impressive, as contemporary pictures show. In 1866 the depth of the platforms was more than doubled by digging out the tracks and later an island platform was made on the southern side of the shed to give the facility for more through trains. Soon, all kinds of structures, from bookshops to barbers' shops, footbridges to signal cabins, sprang up to clutter the platforms. Only in recent years has it recovered some of that early gracious space.

1906, of the King Edward Rail Bridge, to the west of the station, relieved much of that pressure and it became the main route for the East Coast Main Line. The principal use of the High Level Bridge today is to take the Sunderland and Middlesbrough trains, but in the electrification of the East Coast Main Line (ECML), specially-designed pylons were made for it so that it can still take any type of modern train.

Central Station has had to change rather more than the High Level. The appearance of the frontage of the main station block remains little changed today, but additions were made to its western end in 1873, with a large carriage shed running alongside Forth Banks. This building had originally been put up as part of Forth Goods Station in the early 1850s, but when that was rearranged it

The view of Central Station from the Keep, 1955. A V Class tank engine pulls out across the diamond crossing, once said to be the greatest in the world, while a coast-bound electric train waits to leave from the covered platforms of Tynemouth Square.

was carefully dismantled and re-erected at Central Station. Later, offices were added on top and an imposing Revenue Office placed at the Neville Street end. The present screen wall between this and the original Dobson facade was built in 1906, when the 'horse docks' were roofed over.

The addition to the east end, the Central Station Hotel, was rather more substantial. In his original plans, Dobson had included a small hotel block adjoining the station, but, instead, a set of rooms at its east end had been adapted in the name of economy. This was less than satisfactory and, in 1863, the NER built a

proper hotel block, partly based on Dobson's original scheme. Although more modestly decorated than the station facade, it was of a similar style and a matching height. It survives today, but is rather overwhelmed by the extensions built in 1892. This not only added a whole new hotel block to the east, but later two floors were built on top of the original building, making it visually a less well-matched neighbour to the station it serves. However, some of the interiors were stunning , with exuberant use of rich tiling, some of which can still be seen.

A thorough remodelling of the train shed took place at the end of the nineteenth century. The eastern bays served the traffic to the suburbs and towns of north Tyneside and their expansion was becoming difficult to handle. A whole new complex, 'Tynemouth Square', was built with a new roof, platforms, offices and entrances to form what was effectively a station within a station. On the southern side of Central, more land was taken and Forth Street realigned to its present location, enabling the construction of two extra roof spans to the three built originally, enlarging the station considerably. Here a central island platform was built, complete with waiting rooms and offices and a footbridge to connect it to the main concourse whilst the existing platforms were rearranged. The whole scheme was complete by 1894 and essentially the structure of the main station was in the form seen today. At the same time, the bridges and viaduct to Manors were doubled in

The L&NER Railway Magazine *of 1936 illustrated Central's modern open-plan booking hall. Five years earlier, the station had pioneered the use of mechanised ticket machines.*

Gresley's A3 Pacific **Grand Parade** *at Central about 1938. The sister to* **Flying Scotsman***, she has been beautifully presented for a prestigious LNER service.*

Royal Station Hotel today. The 1863 block, corner right, is overwhelmed by the extensions of the 1890s, the assembly somewhat reducing the massive dignity of Central's facade.

width to take four tracks, so developing the famous 'diamond crossing' to the High Level Bridge at the eastern end of the station approaches.

Its character changed with the opening of the King Edward Rail Bridge in 1906. Until then, all the trains on the London-Edinburgh main line had to use the High Level Bridge, so forming a 'Y' shaped route into the station. Every train had to draw in and 'reverse' out, entailing a change of locomotive. When the new bridge came into use to the west of the station, through traffic was possible, reducing delays and engine movements and allowing much more flexibility. This end of the station was partly extended and remodelled; in commemoration of the bridge's opening, a portrait bust of the King was added to the main entrance between those of his parents, Victoria and Albert.

In many ways this was the high point of Central Station – most of the changes that followed were to reflect the fact that traffic was falling rather than increasing. The LNER replaced the NER in 1923 but left little mark on the station, nor did the station suffer damage in the Second World War. The creation of a nationalised British Railways in 1948 saw the station through most of the rest of the twentieth century and through a fundamental rethink of the scale of the railway system itself, in the face of increasing competition from roads. These plans included, at one point, the demolition and complete rebuilding of most of the station, but in the face of local opposition these were withdrawn.

The most fundamental changes undertaken were in the creation of the Tyneside Metro, which was to replace the suburban services to South Shields, Tynemouth and north Tyneside. Opened from 1980 onwards, it made much of Tynemouth Square redundant. Its roof cover was reduced, most of the bays filled in to form car parking, and a brand new underground interchange was built. With the withdrawal of local services and the reduction of freight traffic, surplus avoiding lines to the south of the station were rearranged and a through platform with cantilever roof added together with an extension of the footbridge for access.

As the twentieth century century progressed, the station interior had become a mess of platform buildings. Its last 25 years have seen a clearing up of the public spaces and a rearrangement of the rooms. A new focal point was created in 1985, with the innovative

The Keep is still one of Britain's greatest railway vantage points. Central today, compared to the view on page 80, is now wholly electrified, the diamond crossing much simplified and Tynemouth Square has been completely demolished to form the car park seen to the right.

Travel Centre on the main concourse, allowing the old Booking Office area to be reused for retail. The roofs were refurbished, stonework restored and cleaned and facilities modernised. Recently the false ceilings and wall cladding of the Buffet have been removed to reveal again the Victorian decorative tiling. The effect is stunning.

The train shed now looks very much more open, although it was necessary to fit pylons and cables for the electrification of the main line in 1991. With the privatisation of rail services, Central Station once again serves a number of companies. Spectacular when opened over 150 years ago, it remains one of the grandest and most attractive stations in the country.

Both Central Station and the High Level Bridge had a significant impact on the the development of Newcastle. As the major road and rail focus, it made the area surrounding the station and bridge approaches the most convenient business location. As the reinvigoration of the town continued through the nineteenth century, many grand offices were constructed on Mosley Street, Collingwood Street, St Nicholas' and Westgate Road, including the ornate Union Club, Post Office headquarters and the Mining Institute.

The travel centre, Metro entrance and main concourse, from a similar viewpoint to that on page 79.

Had the crossing of the Tyne been made as planned at Bill Quay, and Greenesfield Station at Gateshead retained as the main station how would Tyneside have looked now? It is to the credit of Newcastle council that they recognised in the 1840s the importance of the railway to the town and insisted on a road-rail bridge serving a town centre station.

To appreciate the context of these vital decisions takes only a climb to the top of the Castle Keep. Dramatically laid out before you stand Greenesfield, Stephenson's bridge, Central Station and the viaduct. Imagine this same view in 1850, stripped of the modern high-rises and the Tyne Bridge, and some idea of Hudson's ambition and Newcastle's determination becomes clear.

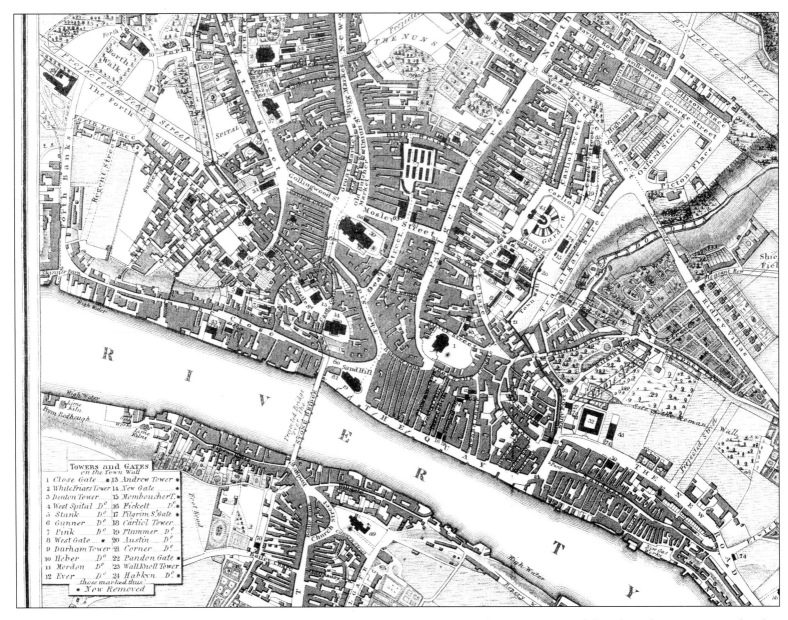

A detail from Thomas Oliver's map of Newcastle and Gateshead, 1830. The Stone Bridge is the only Tyne crossing and the railways have yet to arrive, but the land west of Spital, at the top left, is unbuilt and will form the site of Central Station.

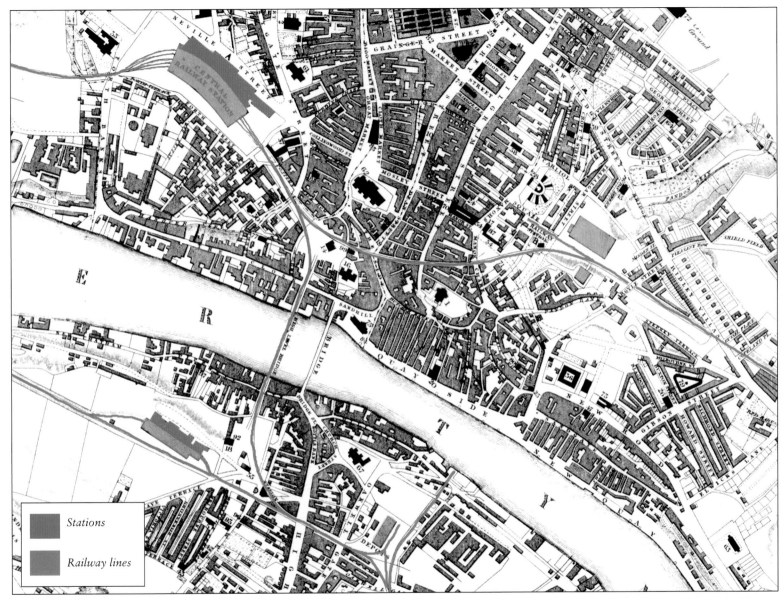

Oliver's 1851 map gives an idea of the extent of changes made to the two towns by railway building. Picked out here in green, the stations of Central and Manors in Newcastle, Greenesfield and Oakwellgate in Gateshead. The railway lines south of the river show the Redheugh Incline linking the Brandling Railway, east, with the Newcastle & Carlisle to the west. In Newcastle, the Carlisle line also runs in from the left to Central where the rail interchange takes the lines east to Edinburgh and North Shields along the great viaduct, or swings south to Darlington across the new High Level Bridge.

The Network Grows: Tyneside Railways 1845-1900

With the completion of the High Level Bridge and Central Station, Newcastle had finally achieved its ambition as the rail centre for the region. One immediate effect was the closure of the almost-new Greenesfield Station in 1850. Located at the west of the High Level at the Gateshead end, it had become sidetracked when the main line went east. It was extended and converted into a workshop for locomotive repairs. In its place, Dobson designed a modest little station on the bridge approaches – never again would Gateshead have pretensions as a major passenger interchange.

Newcastle consolidated its hold with further ambitious building. The Newcastle & North Shields Railway had substantial traf-

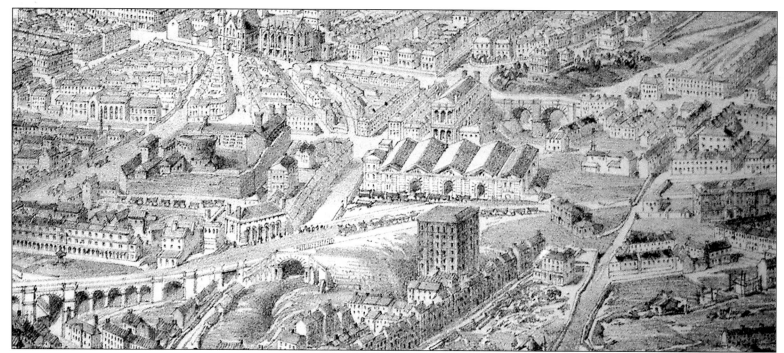

A rare view of Manors, c.1865, from 'Newcastle in the Reign of Queen Victoria' by J. Storey. Bottom left, Manor Chare viaduct leads up to Dobson's Manors Station, with the old Carliol Square terminus, curiously unconnected, behind. To the right, the tall Pandon Dene corn warehouse and the great Trafalgar goods shed, behind which is the New Bridge over Pandon Burn and the recently opened Picton House, terminus of the Blyth & Tyne Railway.

fic with a very convenient, if temporary, station at Manors. When
Hudson took over the company in 1845, he commissioned Dobson
to construct a new Manors Station. This was a distinguished design
in stone, Italian Renaissance in style, with arcading and rusticated
corners. Close by was erected a goods station at Trafalgar, again
designed in the classical style by Dobson and stone built, with a
five span roof supported by iron columns. Like most of Hudson's
commissions, it was generously planned; it proved large enough to
serve as the main goods station for northern traffic for nearly 60
years.

The Fall of the Railway King

By the middle 1840s, George Hudson had reached the height of his
success. The major building schemes he had initiated –
Greenesfield, Central and Manors Stations, High Level Bridge and
viaduct, Trafalgar Goods Yard – were achieved through the firm
hold he had established on the major North Eastern rail routes. In
1843 his Newcastle & Darlington Junction Railway (N&DJR) had
taken over the DJR, followed by the Brandling in 1845 and the
Durham & Sunderland, Great North of England and P&SS the
following year, all then amalgamated into a new York & Newcastle
Railway which controlled the routes south. To the north, his
Newcastle and Berwick Railway (N&BR) had absorbed the
Newcastle and North Shields Railway (N&NSR). All these groups
then combined in 1847 with the formation of the York, Newcastle
& Berwick Railway. He was Chairman of the Midland Railway
and other companies, MP for Sunderland and in every sense
deserved his nickname of 'The Railway King'. His financial muscle,
political acumen and personal drive had transformed the railways
of the North East from a group of squabbling, and frequently
barely viable, independent companies into an integrated rail
system, with a logical infrastructure and buildings to rival any in
the country.

*George Hudson, from a portrait in Monkwearmouth Station. He kept his
support in Sunderland – and role as their MP – long after his disgrace in
the rest of the country. 'When all had forsaken me, Sunderland has
remained firm to me.'*

He had always run rather close to the wind in his affairs, paying dividends from the capital in some of his companies whilst fid-
dling the books. This was not just for personal gain, it was the
financial rocket fuel that many of the major railway projects needed to stimulate investment and Hudson, for all his faults, was the
greatest promoter of the greatest age in the development of the
railway. When the stock market took a tumble and a slump began,

Hudson was found out and the bubble of confidence in him burst. First his railway chairmanships were stripped from him, later he was forced by debt to flee the country.

If one figure deserves a statue in Central Station it is George Hudson. Gladstone said of him after his fall, 'It is a great mistake to look back upon him as a speculator. He was a man of great dis-

Off the rails. Punch's *cartoon of 1849 revelled in the dethronement of the* 'Railway King'.

cernment, possessing a great deal of courage and rich enterprise … a very bold, and not at all an unwise projector.' He never saw the grand opening of the High Level Bridge or of Central Station, but there is no doubt that it was his drive and the confidence he instilled that had been at the core of both projects.

His swashbuckling personal empire was replaced by a more sober regime which looked for sensible economy and sound business management – few of the area's railway buildings of the following 150 years would follow Hudson's desire for ambitious architecture on a grand scale. An exception was the Forth Goods Station built between 1852-54. It was built by the N&CR on land to the west of Central Station; a substantial structure designed by Peter Tate which, in a more modest fashion, had similarities with Dobson's Manors Station.

The Carlisle railway had remained independent from Hudson's great agglomeration of companies. His York Newcastle & Berwick (YN&B) became a constituent part of the newly-formed North Eastern Railway in 1854, and this new company increased its stranglehold on local routes; in 1862 it finally managed to capture the N&C. The major local line to escape them was the Blyth & Tyne Railway. This had developed from the privately-owned Seghill Railway, which principally served to link several North Tyneside pits with the staiths at Percy Main and Seaton Sluice. As such, its main traffic was coal, but some passengers were also carried, mainly miners to and from work. From 1847 it was known as the Blyth & Tyne, being formally constituted as a public company in 1852. Throughout its life, it would carry vast amounts of coal but it also developed its local passenger services to the north of Newcastle and east to the coast. It was a notably well-run company, profitable, efficient and determined to expand. By 1864 it had routes to Blyth, Bedlington, Morpeth and a new line serving the coast via Jesmond, Gosforth, then curving east to Long Benton, Cullercoats and Tynemouth. It formed a Newcastle terminus at New Bridge Street

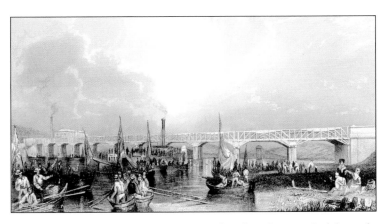

Above, the first wooden N&CR Scotswood Bridge of 1839, which burned down in in 1860, from J.W. Carmichael's 'Views on the Newcastle and Carlisle Railway' and, right, the double-track replacement of 1871.

Owls on the line!

From the *Newcastle Journal*, 23 December 1848

'As the mail train upon the York, Newcastle, and Berwick Railway was proceeding north one night last week, and when near to the station at Cramlington, a party of horned owls, being disturbed in their roost by the noise, made a furious attack upon the engine and those in charge of it. The fireman, while seated in the locomotive, was furiously assailed, and before he could discover the character of his foe, was seriously pecked in the face, and had one of his teeth forced out of its place.'

in an existing Dobson building known as Picton House, and close to the NER station at Manors.

The successful expansion of local services by the B&T, together with their competing Newcastle terminus, were proving stiff competition to the NER's domination of the area's railways. In 1874 they succeeded in taking it over, although it kept its name and identity for many more years. Control of Tyneside was complete nine years later when they gained control of the Scotswood, Newburn & Wylam Railway, a short line of just six-and-a-half miles that served the north bank of the Tyne from Central Station. Opened between 1875 and 1876, it had never been a financial success; it is remembered today principally for its fine bow string bridge at West Wylam and from part of its trackway following the old Wylam waggonway route past the birthplace of George Stephenson. At Scotswood itself, the original timber N&CR bridge crossing the Tyne rather embarrassingly burnt down in 1860 while undergoing tests for the Board of Trade. A temporary crossing was quickly put up, but it was eleven more years until a permanent replacement was opened.

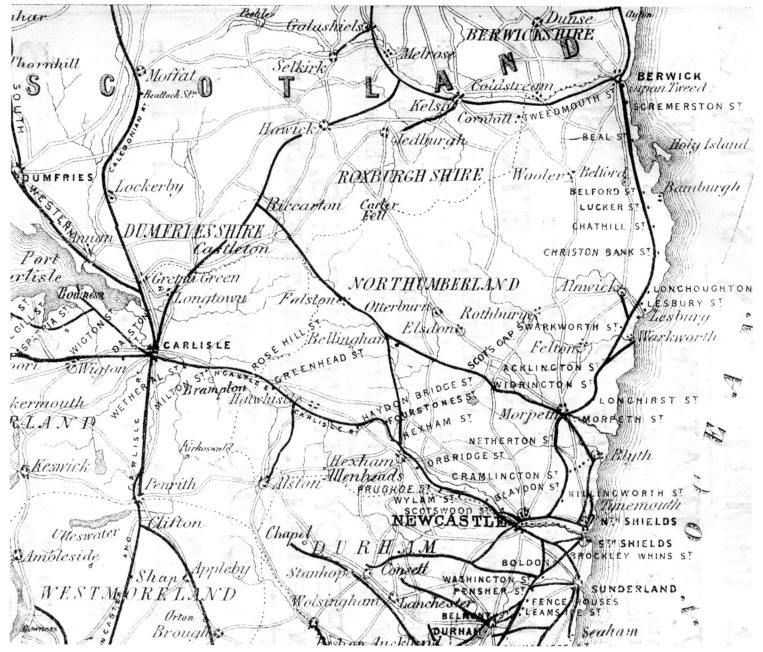

Reid's Railway Guide for 1863. The Blyth & Tyne have yet to bring their route from Tynemouth across to Picton House, the ECML still goes via Leamside and the Wear at Sunderland remains unbridged, but the passenger routes are becoming well developed. Reid's of Newcastle were to build a considerable business from their railway guides, the first of which came out as early as 1849.

Tynemouth Station, from a postcard sent from North Shields to Carlisle around 1905. The station was noted for its colourful floral displays during the summer holiday season – and for its unusual arched footbridge.

After the intense building programme of the late 1840s and early 1850s, the remainder of the nineteenth century saw a more gentle expansion of the Tyneside rail network as it adapted to the rapidly increasing traffic and the population growth of the area itself. It has already been seen how Central Station was rearranged to take this into account, particularly with the local services to north Tyneside and the suburbs of Newcastle. Initially these were based on the old N&NS line to Tynemouth via Manors, extended in 1879 by the 'Riverside Railway' which gave a southern loop nearer the Tyne at Byker, Walker and Percy Main.

With the acquisition of the B&TR in 1874, the NER were in control of the more northerly local line from New Bridge Street

Station via Benton to Tynemouth. The old company had already replaced its original Tynemouth terminus with a new building to the east in 1865. In 1882 the NER built a whole new line nearer to the coast to better serve Whitley Bay and Cullercoats, joined it to their North Shields route and built a very impressive new station for Tynemouth. Reflecting the holiday industry of the town, itself made possible by the railway, it had nine platforms covered overall with an iron-supported glass canopy nearly 600 feet long. The fittings were of high quality throughout to produce a delightful train shed, with the long road frontage in a Venetian style of brick and stone. It was, and fortunately still is, the apogee of late Victorian station design – Tyneside's last grand public building from the great

Looking over Greenesfield towards the High Level Bridge, c.1868, contrasting with Thomas Hair's 1845 view on page 65.

the opening of the Derwent Valley Line to Blackhill in 1867 and the rebuilding of the Consett Line via Beamish. To the east, the new Tyne Dock had been completed in 1859 and was served by the NER with a complex of lines. It was augmented in 1872 with a major new passenger route, the Jarrow Branch, which formed a route between Gateshead and South Shields, avoided the congested loop of the original Brandling Line and serving Hebburn and Jarrow.

The track leading east of Central Station carried both the main line to Berwick and the local North Tyneside trains; severe congestion led it to be expanded to four tracks in 1894, necessitating the widening of the entire viaduct to Manors. At Heaton, where the routes diverged, a large marshalling yard was established, principally as a depot for carriages feeding Central Station, but with most of the loco-

age of the railway.

South of the Tyne a number of branches and modifications were made by the NER. The main line to London was rerouted in 1868 to run through Team Valley and Chester-le-Street, cutting off the long loop made by the old Leamside line and giving a direct run to Durham – this is substantially the same route used by the ECML today. It led to the replacement, that same year, of the small Gateshead Station, built by Dobson, with a larger building near the High Level Bridge, Gateshead West, although its architecture might best be described as modest and workmanlike. To the south and west of Gateshead, the traffic generated by the growing pit villages was tapped by a host of extensions and improvements, including

motives stored at Greenesfield. Here, the short-lived but impressive station had been converted and extended, at first to a workshop for locomotive repairs for the York, Newcastle & Berwick Railway (YN&BR), with its hotel building used as offices for the Superintendent. With the formation of the NER it became the main engine-building works for the railway, extended several times until it covered the entire available site with workshops, assembly areas and engine storage sheds.

Greenesfield was not the only locomotive works in the area; Robert Stephenson & Co. were still at their cramped South Street site in Newcastle with Hawthorn's next door and (until 1896) Black, Hawthorn & Co. at Gateshead, all producing engines for the home and export markets. At Walker, a carriage and waggon-building works was developed for the NER, at Blaydon, sheds for locomotives working the North British, Carlisle and Derwent Valley routes. Percy Main was the old depot for the B&T, the NER adding to it locomotive, carriage and waggon repair shops; Tyne Dock shedded freight trains and local engines whilst in Gateshead, Borough Gardens supplied shunting and freight locomotives.

There was now a comprehensive network of national, regional and local services on Tyneside, but that was only part of the impact that the railways had on the area. Freight formed over half of the business of the NER, particularly coal working in the North East, but also general goods, specialised engineering movements, parcels and post. Just west of Central Station, the Forth Goods Yard was completely rebuilt between 1867 and 1874, the old building being reconstructed at the station and replaced by a large and attractive complex designed by Thomas Prosser, extended again in the early 1890s. The Trafalgar and Forth yards were two of the most impressive goods areas, but most of the stations in the rail network had some combination of sidings, sheds and coal yards. Near the staiths, such as Percy Main and Tyne Dock, were huge marshalling yards, and colliery railways were found all along Tyneside, many of them privately owned, and with their own sheds, repair works and network of sidings. The cargo docks, quarries, major engineering and manufacturing works, shipyards, gas plants and, later, generating stations were connected to the system. Dedicated freight lines and branches were built, including the 1870 Quayside Branch in Newcastle, which featured a frighteningly steep descent from the Trafalgar yard down to the river. The main livestock market of Newcastle was next to Forth

Greenesfield works about 1900. The railways had huge staff numbers – in 1924 Central Station alone employed 730 – and it was considered a job for life.

Goods; fish, horses, milk, chickens, even racing pigeons were moved by rail. All over the lacework of lines around Tyneside there was a constant stream of expresses, local trains, heavy and general freight movements, coal waggons, with all that implied in buildings, bridges and level crossings – and manpower. It functioned as the essential transport medium for the region and the nation; the sight and sound of the railway had become an everyday and inescapable backdrop to life in the area.

Ken Hoole Collection

Ken Hoole Collection

Above: this little 0-4-0 tank engine at the Infirmary Yard, Forth Goods, was used to move the waggons around – hence the shunter with his pole for unhitching the couplings – and was typical of the modest, everyday locomotives working throughout the region. It was built by Manning Wardle of Leeds in 1874 as NER 960, but was photographed here in 1889 with its new number.

Above: an 0-6-0 of the Blyth & Tyne Railway at Percy Main waggon shop. It was built in 1860 by Robert Stephenson & Co. to their famous 'long boiler design', a very successful early arrangement dating back to 1841. With its short wheelbase it could work tight curves but had the power to pull heavy loads - a real maid-of-all-work, although mainly used by the B&T for coal haulage.

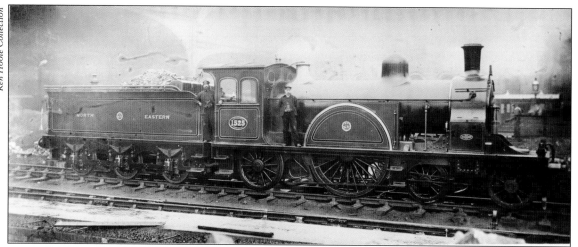

Ken Hoole Collection

Left: the rather more flashy end of the NER. This J Class, with its sister I Class, were the only compound singles built in Britain and designed for express passenger work. Built at Greenesfield in 1890, no. 1525 had just one pair of driving wheels, but of the huge size of 7ft 7½ ins, dwarfing the fireman.

Right: an engine that encapsulates a remarkable range of North East railway history.

This wonderful engine, No. 910, was built at Greensfield to Edward Fletcher's design to haul York-Edinburgh expresses. Brand new in 1875, it ran in the S&DR Jubilee procession of that year, and again, just retired, at the 1925 Centenary (*below right*).

At the 1975 celebration it was pulled by *Flying Scotsman*, making it the only engine to have appeared in all the commemorations of George Stephenson's line.

Part of the NRM's collection, it is on display at Darlington North Road alongside *Locomotion*.

Edward Fletcher served as an apprentice at Robert Stephenson & Co where he was involved with building *Rocket* and drove *Invicta* at the opening of George and Robert Stephenson's Canterbury & Whitstable railway in 1830. After serving on the Newcastle & Darlington Junction railway of George Hudson, he became the first locomotive superintendent of the new NER from 1854.

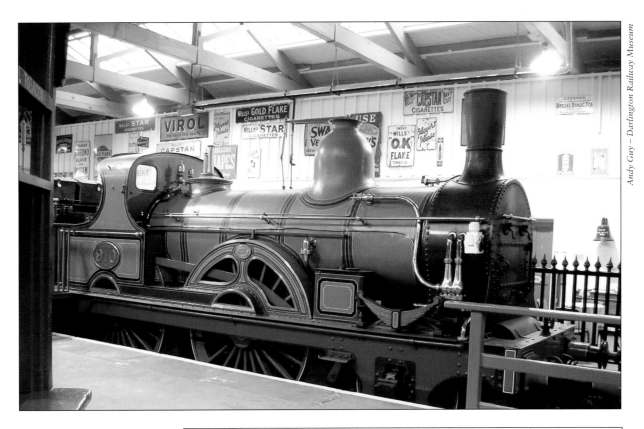

Andy Guy – Darlington Railway Museum

Ken Hoole Collection

The NER and the High Level were powerful symbols in the North East, as shown in this advertisement for boot polish from the early twentieth century. Pelaw, on the South Shields line, had a massive Co-operative factory.

From Glory to Crisis – Tyneside Railways 1900-1948

Tyneside entered the new century with a comprehensive rail system on a mighty scale. The next ten years saw a significant reorganisation of two of its major passenger routes. When the main line south had been rerouted via Team Valley in 1868, it had been intended to carry it across the Tyne on a new bridge just west of Central Station to relieve the heavy traffic using the High Level. However, there was no money to be found for it, and the Forth Goods Yard blocked the only practical route. It was to be over 30 years until the decision was made to build and by then the situation had become critical. Not only was it awkward that all

trains on the ECML had to enter and leave at the east end of Central, but with the main engine sheds at Gateshead, relieved and relieving locomotives had to use the High Level for access. It was bottlenecked; delays were frequent and working was increasingly inefficient. The NER finally bit the bullet, agreed the essential need for a new crossing, and accepted that the recently rebuilt Forth Goods buildings would have to be chopped through.

The foundation stone for the King Edward Bridge was laid in July 1902 and the bridge was completed just over four years later. The original design, of two great spans tied to land approach

Left, the King Edward VII Bridge under construction, using a unique pulley system to transport materials. Right, King Edward opens the bridge, 1906.

arches, had to be abandoned when old coal workings were found on the banks; it was built instead with four steel lattice spans, each up to 300 feet long supported on piers of Norwegian granite. The total cost came to over half a million pounds, but it thoroughly modernised railway working over the Tyne. Now that Central had a river crossing to the west, through trains on the ECML became possible for the first time, and, with the rail link between the two bridge approaches on the south bank, there was a complete circular route which gave not only great flexibility for traffic movements, but relieved the excessive use of the High Level. The King Edward is not a beautiful bridge – sturdy and workmanlike are perhaps the best that can be said of it – but a century later it still carries the main burden of trains crossing the Tyne.

A postcard commemorating the opening of the Tynemouth electric railway. The system was introduced to compete with the popular street trams.

The first threat to the supremacy of the railway was seen in 1901, when Newcastle's electric tram service was started. Much more efficient than the old horse-drawn trams, it proved highly popular; the system rapidly grew throughout the city and suburbs and along the Tyneside towns. In some places, such as Park Road in Wallsend and along the Coxlodge in High Heaton, it followed the disused track of the old waggonways, an irony little appreciated by the NER, which correctly saw the urban tram system as very real competition to its local services – passenger numbers dropped from nearly 10 million in 1901 to 5.8 million just two years later. It responded with a thorough reorganisation of its North Tyneside

routes. Early in 1904, it replaced steam on the New Bridge Street-Benton line with an electrical train service taking power from a third rail, quickly extended along the whole local system from Central to Tynemouth, North Shields and the Riverside Branch. It was a bold move, one of the very early overground electrical rail networks and the first in the country to be used for freight – the steep Quayside line was electrified at the same time (one of the two original locomotives is preserved at the NRM in York). Quiet, clean and fast, the new trains proved very successful with the public, while the NER found them to be economical and reliable.

The major problem was the short gap – only a few hundred yards – between the terminus at New Bridge Street and Manors,

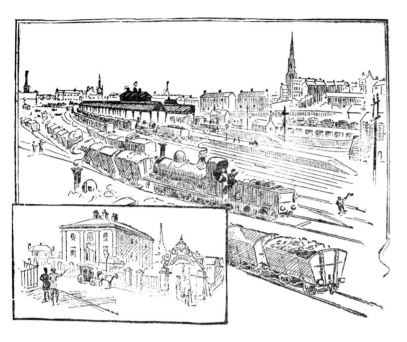

In April 1901, the Newcastle Weekly Journal *reported on the plans for* Picton Square *and* New Bridge Street *as the Manors gap was considered.*

New Bridge Street Goods in the 1930s. *Of advanced reinforced concrete, this 1906 building was considered 'absolutely fireproof' when built, but the bombing in 1941 was another matter. It was largely destroyed.*

preventing a circular route. In the way was the Trafalgar Goods Yard and Dobson's Manors Station and, just as at Forth, the railway directors had the unenviable task of demolishing their own property. In 1909 this expensive gap was plugged, goods traffic transferred to a fresh site at New Bridge Street and an interchange, known as Manors North, built, although from 1917 all services were started from the Tynemouth Square platforms at Central.

The new route enabled a flexible and efficient local service, which included regular expresses. It regained some of the passenger traffic lost to the trams, but suffered a severe setback in 1918 when the Walkergate depot for the electric sets suffered a disastrous fire. A completely new set of sheds was built at South Gosforth. They are now the main depot for the Tyneside Metro. Here was a junction that led to the Ponteland Branch, opened in 1905 and later

extended to Darras Hall, but the line proved to have disappointing revenues and was closed to passengers in 1929.

Early in the century, the position of Tyneside as a major builder of locomotives suffered two crushing blows. In 1902, Robert Stephenson's left their historic but cramped site in South Street, Forth for a brand new factory in Darlington, although many of their buildings were taken over by their neighbouring engine makers, Hawthorn, Leslie. In Gateshead, the Greenesfield works was the town's largest employer with over 3,000 men. It was a great shock to the town when, in 1910, the manufacturing of new locomotives was moved, again to Darlington, and again due to a shortage of space. The works continued for engine repairing until 1932. Brighter news came in 1919, when Armstrong & Co. of Elswick started large-scale locomotive-building, but Tyneside never regained the major role it had held since the first years of the railway steam engine.

PRIVATE LOCOMOTIVE BUILDERS

The first factory in the world to be established with the intention to build locomotives was Robert Stephenson's in Newcastle in 1823. Its products were to include *Locomotion* and *Rocket*, then the *Planet* and 'long boiler' designs that would feature at the opening of many of the early railways, not just in Britain but on the mainland of Europe, in the USA and Canada. Next to their South Street works was the engineering company of Robert and William Hawthorn who began the production of locomotives in 1832. In the great railway boom of the 1830s and 1840s, these two firms would be major suppliers to the new companies.

They were not the only local constructors. When locomotive

building was still more of a light industry, making relatively simple engines, several other firms tried their hands at it, including the Thompson Brothers at Newburn and Michael Longridge at Bedlington, but as the product became more complex and capital-intensive in the second half of the nineteenth century, the smaller works abandoned the business. Stephenson's and Hawthorn's dominated, joined in 1865 by the unrelated firm of Black, Hawthorn and Co. of Gateshead, who had taken over the locomotive business of Ralph Coulthard. The market of these independent builders changed considerably after the mid-1840s. The railway companies had started a process of consolidation that would see the emergence of such empires as the Great Western, Great Northern, NER, Midland, London & North Western – they would build their own engines, as the NER did at its Greenesfield works.

The independent makers did supply them at times of production shortfall, but much

McDowell Trust Collection – Stephenson Locomotive Society

Robert Stephenson & Co, No.4 Machine Shop. This 1902 view gives a vivid impression of the cramped and archaic conditions at South Street.

Armstrong Whitworth's Boiler Erecting Shop with the Russian contract.

Locomotives for the Queensland Railway being loaded on Armstrong's specially built ship.

of their business became the building of locomotives for the private mining, quarrying and heavy industries, together with an important export market.

Black, Hawthorn went into liquidation in 1897; their engine business was taken over by Chapman & Furneaux until its closure just five years later. Stephenson's moved to a new works in Darlington in 1902. In 1937 it combined with Hawthorn's to form Robert Stephenson & Hawthorns, the Newcastle works concentrating on repairs and steam-engine building, with Darlington mainly concerned with diesel and battery-electric engines.

The other main local builder between the wars was Armstrong, Whitworth of Scotswood. Their munitions business was understandably depressed after the First World War, but the heavily damaged railways of Europe offered new opportunities. In 1919 they opened a factory capable of building up to 230 mainline locomotives a year. Almost immediately they won the contract to make 200 heavy freight engines for the Belgian State Railway, at the time the

largest single order for locomotives ever placed. In 1922 they built 200 boilers for the Russian railways and developed a strong export business, to the extent that they built specialised ships to transport the locomotives in running order. They were notably advanced in their thinking, with a large department for diesel and diesel-electric engines, but the advent of war returned the company's attention to munitions – no new locomotives were made by them after 1939.

The cutbacks in the railway network, the conversion from steam and the decline of the heavy industries badly affected the private builders after the war. Stephenson and Hawthorns, by then part of the English Electric group, closed the Newcastle works in 1961, ending a sequence of locomotive building on Tyneside that had begun with the Gateshead engine of 1805.

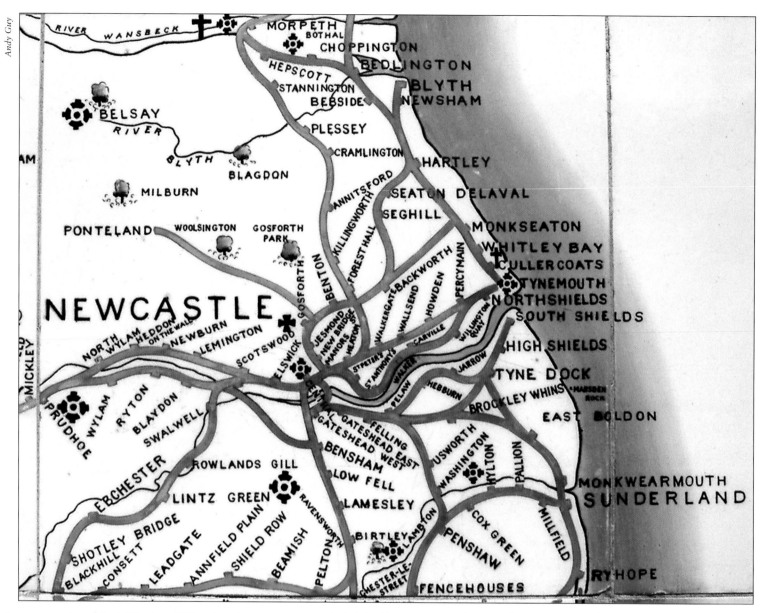

Passenger routes of the NER about 1910, when the system was near its height. Compared to Reid's map of 1863 (page 90), the Tynemouth Loop is complete, the Riverside Branch via Willington Quay has opened, as have the routes to Jarrow, North Wylam and the ECML through Lamesley. The King Edward Bridge has enabled the Central Station 'roundabout' to operate and the Wear has been crossed at Sunderland. These well known tile maps can still be found at Tynemouth and Whitby stations, at the National Railway Museum and in South Shields Museum.

In 1923, the 'grouping' of railway companies resulted in the NER becoming part of the London & North Eastern Railway (LNER). It made little immediate difference to the region, although it would see the introduction of the Gresley Pacific locomotives to the ECML. Engines such as *Mallard* and *Flying Scotsman* would provide perhaps the most memorable scenes of the steam era as they powered the expresses from London to Edinburgh. Speeds of over 100 mph could be maintained over long distances, with one service taking just four hours between Newcastle and Kings Cross. Heaton, meanwhile, was expanded to form the main marshalling yards for passenger traffic.

South Tyneside had always been the Cinderella railway area. Gateshead had two stations, East and West, which were no more than utilitarian and only provided local services. The London main line trains never did, and never would, stop at Gateshead, unlike its counterparts of Sunderland, Stockton, Darlington and Durham – how far it had fallen from the great prospects of the 1840s. Following the success of the electrification of the North Tyneside local services, the NER had proposed to convert the routes to South Shields and Sunderland as well. For over three decades nothing came of their plans, until the LNER finally electrified the line to South Shields in 1938. Even then it principally used old stock from the early 1920s, withdrawn from the Tynemouth circuit when that line was given brand new trains.

The railways of Tyneside suffered relatively little physical damage during World War II. The major casualty was New Bridge Street Goods Station which, with its great corn warehouse, was burned out by bombing in 1941. Heaton too was badly hit, although Greenesfield saw a revival when it was reopened for engine repairs. But the entire national railway system was exhaust-

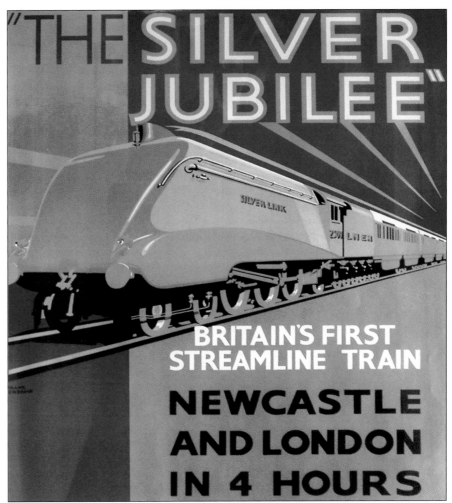

Private collection

The introduction of Gresley's stunning A4 streamline engines in 1935 caused something of a sensation as the LNER tried to break the dour grip of the Depression.

ed by the war. Worn out stock, tired facilities and a desperate lack of investment saw the industry in crisis. In 1948, all the railway companies were nationalised – the era of 'British Railways' had begun.

Before World War I the pride of the North Eastern Railway were the Class Z and Z1 Atlantic (4-4-2) locomotives; examples were built by the NER in Darlington and by the North British Locomotive Co. in Glasgow. Here number 735, one of the Glasgow-built engines crosses the King Edward VII Bridge into Gateshead with a southbound express, c.1912.

Steam and speed. The two simultaneous 10 o'clock departures from Newcastle cross the King Edward VII Bridge over the Tyne, 22 May 1936. On the left is Britain's first all-streamlined train and pride of the LNER, the 'Silver Jubilee' for London, headed by Class A4 locomotive No. 2512 **Silver Fox.** *On the right is a Newcastle to Liverpool express headed by Class A3 locomotive No. 2582* **Sir Hugo.** *Examples of both locomotive types have been preserved, the most famous being* **Mallard** *and the* **Flying Scotsman.**

Modern electric services may be quicker, quieter and cleaner, but they cannot compete with the sheer drama of the steam era.

British Rail and Beyond – Tyneside Railways after 1948

The last half of the twentieth century saw a wholesale reorganisation of the railway system, national and local. Now under a central administration, it was subject to a government policy that vacillated between changing political objectives and the restrictions of a weakening national economy. In its core role as a major transport medium it was increasingly challenged by the growth in road traffic with increasing competition from car, bus and lorry for both passengers and freight. At a time when money was short, yet major investment needed, and when the fixed routes of what was essentially a Victorian railway were proving ill-suited to the changes seen in industry and housing, it was inevitable that some hard decisions were going to have to be made.

The long-term future of the railway was mapped out in 1955, when the Modernisation Plan was unveiled. This proposed a strategic policy by which steam would be replaced by diesel or electric traction, the curse of unbraked freight waggons would be ended to allow fast freight services, signalling updated to coloured lights, mainlines improved and stations brought up to date. The huge investment needed was seldom provided and the situation of British Railways continued to deteriorate. In 1963, Dr Beeching, appointed to take a purely financial view of the system and to stem its massive losses, unveiled his notorious 'Reshaping' plan which proposed the closure of over 2,000

Ken Hoole Collection

1 January 1948 – staff at Central Station celebrate the first day of British Railways.

stations due to their lack of economic viability.

The Beeching Plan only accelerated a process that had started with Nationalisation. Between 1948 and 1971, British Railways lost nearly 60 per cent of its route miles, 67 per cent of its stations and 78 per cent of its freight waggons. With such an overall national reduction in the scale of the railways it was inevitable that Tyneside would suffer severely.

In 1954, the Derwent Valley line to Blackhill was closed to passengers, followed a year later by the Consett route via Beamish. From 1958, closure of stations started on the North Wylam Branch and was completed ten years later. Between 1962 and 1964 the Tanfield Branch was shut down; 1963 was the end of passenger services on the Leamside line; 1964 on the Penshaw and Pelaw; 1965, Monkwearmouth to South Shields; 1973, the Riverside Branch closed on the north bank of the Tyne. These were only some of the more prominent Tyneside victims; Durham and Northumberland saw their local branches comprehensibly removed so that by 1975 the very concept of the rural railway was effectively history.

The area's rail system had withdrawn into its key routes: the East Coast Main Line (ECML) with its national connections; the regional lines to Sunderland, Teesside and Carlisle; the local services to Tyneside. Not only was the choice of routes available from Central Station considerably reduced, but the character of passenger travel changed as well. On the ECML steam was phased out from 1961 with the introduction of diesels; the service was further improved when the High Speed Train came into regular use in 1978. However, when the electricified routes on the South Shields and Tynemouth routes were converted to diesel operation in 1963 and 1967 it was felt by many to be a retrograde step – the trains were slower and noisier and they did nothing to halt the decline in suburban traffic, adding to a general dismay about the deteriorating state of the surviving stations.

A Tyne Improvement Commission engine carries pit props from North Shields Quay in 1954 – the Wear harbours also used their own locomotives.

A deadly disease

The Beeching report contained some sobering statistics. One third of the route miles carried just one per cent of the passenger miles and half of them only four per cent. Half of the passenger stations produced just two per cent of the passenger receipts. Half of the goods stations contributed less than two per cent of the freight revenue.

Such a situation was untenable. Doctor Beeching remains demonised for his subsequent 'axing' of the hopeless routes but that is a view based on sentiment rather than reality. It should be recognised as the clinical diagnosis and treatment of a disease that was crippling the entire rail network.

The industry at nationalisation

At the state take-over in 1948, the railway industry was massive but fragmented. Staff numbered 629,000, often working in primitive conditions, especially maintenance staff and firemen, whilst many facilities were worn out. A stock of over 20,000 locomotives was split into 400 types – plus 8,700 horses. Rationalisation, modernisation and wholesale reduction were to fundamentally change the face of the railway in Tyne and Wear as in the whole country

Left, top to bottom: Forth Goods was once called the largest in the world and freight sheds large and small were found all over the rail network – they have now almost disappeared; an 'atmospheric' scene in the Sunderland Depot, c.1960 – working conditions under steam could be awful; a range of different locomotive types at Borough Gardens shed, 1957.

Sunderland LNER Loco AFC, winners of the LNER League and Cup, 1930-31. Railway employment had dropped to 116,000 by the mid-1990s.

The freight lines saw a similar, if slower, cut back. One of the features of the region's rail network was the remarkable number of colliery lines, often owned and run by the coal companies themselves. Vesting Day, in 1947, saw the nationalisation of the coal industry and the takeover of all these lines by the new National Coal Board. This included the South Shields, Marsden & Whitburn Colliery Railway, which carried passengers as well as coal traffic. Eccentric and somewhat decrepit, the 'Marsden Rattler' abandoned its passenger service in 1953.

County Durham had 133 working pits in 1954 – by 1980, 114 had closed with production concentrated on the coastal strip.

Tyne & Wear Museums ©I.S. Carr

Wideopen in 1973 – an NCB train crosses the old A1. A situation common enough around the region then, but completely unacceptable today.

Northumberland saw a similar process, together with a change to Blyth as the main harbour for exports. As a result, the colliery lines had become largely redundant and the concentration of routes to the Tyneside staiths greatly reduced. At the same time, coke works, town gas plants, coal-fired power stations, ship building and heavy engineering works – all served by the rail system – were in a decline that was often terminal.

This had an inevitable knock-on effect on the entire rail infrastructure of Tyneside. The reduction of routes and the change from steam meant that the system was overburdened with support structures and a rigorous restructuring was undertaken. Gateshead suffered a double blow in 1959 when the Borough Gardens shed was closed and the Greenesfield works greatly reduced – the old station buildings of 1844 were later demolished, although the hotel building still stands. 1963 saw the end of Heaton as a major depot; two years later Gateshead West station shut; the following year Blaydon

NEDC

Tyne Marshalling Yards about 1963. The site has seen a resurgence with the recent growth in freight traffic.

The last train leaves Willington Quay, 20 July 1973, as the Riverside Branch closes.

shed was closed and later demolished; 1966 saw the demolition of Percy Main shed; 1967, closure of the remains of the war-damaged New Bridge Street Goods Yard; Tyne Dock shed went in 1970 and 1972 saw the demolition of Forth Street Goods. An environment where the impact of the railway was ever present – the great sheds and local station yards, the overbridges, level crossings, signal boxes, staiths – had been mainly swept away.

There was rebuilding as well as demolition. A modern freightliner depot was built on the Penshaw-Pelaw line, the Tyne Marshalling Yards opened in the Team Valley and Borough Gardens became the site of the new Tyneside Freight Depot. The greatest project was the creation of the Metro, not just as an update of tired local systems, but a pioneering attempt to reconsider the role of the modern urban railway.

In 1970, the Tyneside Passenger Transport Authority (PTA) was established by the government as the guiding force for local policies on public transport. With the PT Executive as its professional arm, it took over the Newcastle and South Shields corporation buses

and, in 1973, the local rail services. For the first time the future of the area's rail services was within the power of local government rather than railway organisations. From several options, including the closure of the suburban lines, studies favoured the creation of a 'Light Rapid Transit' system, a combination of the light railway with the tram and the underground.

Although much of the route was to be based on the existing British Railway lines of the Tynemouth loop and the South Shields branch, the most exciting innovation was four miles of tunnel under the centres of Newcastle and Gateshead, with new bridges over the Tyne and Ouseburn. Although Manors and Central Station had plenty of capacity, they were on the fringes of the city centre and not particularly convenient, whilst the underground route allowed stations in the very heart of the city at Haymarket, Monument and St James. Considerable underpinning of buildings was necessary, with foundation problems at Central and the unexpected discovery of ancient mine workings in Gateshead. New stations were created where necessary, old ones were revitalised or rebuilt. The Ponteland line, abandoned for passenger working back in 1929, was reconstructed to serve the growing north western suburbs and the South Gosforth sheds became both the new depot and the central operations centre.

The first stage, Haymarket to Tynemouth, was opened in 1980 after six years of construction work with the rest of the route following as it was completed. The bridge over the Tyne, the Queen Elizabeth II, is made of trussed steel with fabricated box chords and has three spans supported on concrete columns. It is simple but surprisingly handsome, while the curving Byker viaduct over Ouseburn, over 2,600 feet long, is strikingly modern. The old Manors North Station, a dingy and depressing place by the 1970s, was demolished and replaced, while the south bank of the Tyne really benefitted by the renewal of the line, added facilities and fresh stations, particularly the new underground station at

Ken Hoole Collection

The huge hole in the ground that was to be the Gateshead Metro Station, June 1976.

Gateshead Station (later Gateshead East) in its glory days at the turn of the nineteenth century. This entrance and arched arcade on the approach to the High Level still remains.

Gateshead. There was, however, one line on the Tyneside system that did not survive. The loop via Walker and Willington Quay had ever-falling passenger numbers and a collection of worn-out stations. In 1973, after a new access road had been built alongside the route, the PTE closed the Riverside Branch.

The Metro has proved a great success with some 33 million journeys taken each year and its example has since been followed by other major urban areas as they have sought to modernise local travel. Nor has the mainline railway stood still. In 1987, a station at the Gateshead MetroCentre retail complex was opened on the Newcastle-Carlisle line, with direct routes from Darlington, Middlesbrough and Sunderland. It is a sign of the times that a shopping centre on the outskirts is now served by the regional train services but Gateshead itself is not – it lost its overground station with the formation of the Tyneside Metro. Gateshead West closed

in 1965 and Gateshead East in 1981.

On the ECML, the electrification, first mooted by the NER early in the century, was finally carried out and the service opened in 1991. Privatisation of the rail system in the mid-1990s proved highly controversial but there is no doubt that the railways have seen a considerable increase in both freight and passenger traffic, to the extent that some lines might be reopened to relieve the pressure on the main routes. On Tyneside, the rail system has seen a vast improvement from the dire depths it had sunk to in the 1970s. It now seems to have a secure future and holds the promise of improved services, but there can be little doubt that the dominant role that the railway used to play in the transport of the region is not likely to be repeated.

The station excavation and tunnels at Manors, 1977. The scale of the works needed for the Metro are now barely apparent to the passenger.

Tyneside Tunnels

The Metro is recognised as Tyneside's 'underground' but it was not its first – there were three earlier 'subterranean railways' that were quite remarkable in their day.

'Kitty's Drift' was named after colliery engineer Christopher ('Kitty') Bedlington, viewer of the East Kenton pit to the north of Newcastle. In 1796 he built a tunnel from the deep coal seams down to the Tyne staiths at Scotswood, enabling him to drain the mine and also transport the coal by rail directly to the riverside. It produced perhaps the most evocative – and strangest – description of travel on the old colliery waggonways:

A Journey down Kitty's Drift

From *The Picture of Newcastle*, 1807

'… some of the men, who know of your coming, will assist in seating you on a set of small empty coal waggons, capable of containing two persons each, seven of which are drawn along a railway by one horse. As soon as you are placed, with your candles lighted, you set off at full speed, with a boy in the first waggon, for your charioteer, into a tunnel, or subterraneous passage six feet high, about the same breadth, and three miles in length. You will find it an advantage to have one of the men for a guide, to point out anything, that may appear striking on your passage to the pit. It is particularly necessary to guard against putting your hands suddenly out of the waggon, as the tunnel, in most places, is only wide enough to admit the waggon and horses, and you are of course by doing so in danger of receiving an injury; but if you sit undisturbed, you ascend very smoothly and pleasantly up the tunnel, on an inclined plane, till you arrive at the place where the men are working the coals. At your first entrance into the tunnel you are struck with the noise of the waggons, which, being fastened with chains to each other, and going at the rate of ten miles an hour, make a reverberatory noise resembling thunder. The passage is in general hewn out of solid rock, composed of what miners call a metal stone, a sort of schistus. Where there is no rock, it is arched with brick or stone.

The water from the pit runs down by the side of the railway to the river. The waggons are deep and square; wider at the top, than at the bottom, and are fast on all sides. The bottom has hinges, and can be let down to discharge the coals, of which these waggons contain about three bolls each. At intervals there are double railways; and where you come to one of these, the boy stops his horse, and a dead silence ensues, forming a striking contrast to the noise you have just heard. After calling aloud, he listens to hear if any loaden waggons are coming down, that they may there pass each other. The candle of the boy coming down appears like a star at a distance through the gloom, and has a very pleasing effect, as it gradually approaches.

When he is past, your driver renews his speed, until he reaches the next interval, when he repeats his call, and should no answer be heard in return, he proceeds. If, by the negligence of the boys, the waggons should meet, where there is no double railway, the boy with the empty waggons unlooses his horse, which is taught to turn round, and force the waggons back with its breast, until they reach the double part. The full ones having passed you, you set forward again … The air up the tunnel is cold, but perfectly pure. Your approach to the workings is announced by a sensible warmness. You alight from your waggon … East Kenton pit is so much more easy of access than others, from its being the only one, which you can enter by a tunnel or railway, that it has been visited by many ladies. It is usual to recompense the waggon boy, and any of the men to whom you give any trouble, with a few shillings each.'

Kitty's Drift ran the quite extraordinary length of three miles. Similar tunnels had been built in Britain and on the continent to move minerals from the seams to the surface, but the mine-owners had principally used them for canals. Bedlington's Drift was the longest rail tunnel in Britain until the Woodhead opened in 1845 and the first of any great length to be purpose-built.

Kitty's had, by then, been long closed. A roof fall blocked the line in 1810, although it continued in use as a drain until the pit closed in 1857. The exact route is now lost; it is likely that the river exit was covered when the approaches to the Scotswood Bridge were built. However another similar tunnel does still exist, largely intact, running through the heart of Newcastle.

Leazes Main Colliery was at Spital Tongues, on the southern edge of the Town Moor. Between the pits and the staiths by the Ouseburn lay the centre of Newcastle – a surface waggonway was plainly impractical. Instead, the colliery dug the 'Victoria Tunnel', under what is now the Hancock Museum, then curving down below New Bridge Street to emerge near the Tyne by Glasshouse Bridge, a length of a mile and a half. Reaching a maximum depth of 85 feet, the tunnel is in the form of a brick-lined arch through clay, with the bed formed of sandstone blocks. The rails were made

The Victoria Tunnel, 1939.

of wood topped by iron plates, carrying unusually long and narrow waggons necessary to clear the roof. Twenty were sent down at once, with a stationary engine to haul back the empties.

The tunnel closed in 1857, the same year that Kitty's Drift was

The tunnel, photographed in 1975, was refitted as an air raid shelter during World War II with entrances in the city centre.

finally abandoned. In the Second World War it found a new use as an air-raid shelter and now, still generally in good condition, it carries sewer pipes along some of its length. In 1870 the roof was broken into during the construction of the third of Tyneside's 'undergrounds'.

The Quayside Branch was built principally in tunnels and cuttings to form a connection between the riverside and the main line near Manors Station, a distance of just under a mile. The gradient was fearsome, as much as 1 in 27 in part, and that, combined with the line's steep curves, was at the very limit of a steam engine's abilities. In 1904, two electric locomotives took over, replaced by diesels

in 1964. The Branch closed five years later, but is still remembered as one of the ultimate tests of the adhesion locomotive – and an extreme demonstration of the principles tested at the Wylam waggonway nearly 200 years ago.

A scene on the Quayside, sketched by R.J.S. Bertram in 1914. This part of the riverside is now so redeveloped that it is hard to realise that it formed a busy industrial area. The little tank engines were used just for shunting, leaving the heavy tunnel work to the electric locomotives.

Railways on Wearside

The general history of the railways in the Wearside and Sunderland area of Tyne and Wear was similar in outline to that of Tyneside, although on a somewhat smaller scale. Here, too, was an early concentration of coal waggonways to supply the colliers, followed by the growth of local railways and the core problem of bridging a major river. But the timing and character of these developments was quite different.

On the Tyne, colliers were blocked from sailing upstream only by the stone bridge at Newcastle. However, the Wear was a shallower river and the colliers could hardly pass much beyond the river entrance at Sunderland, nor was it deep enough to take keels past Lambton. With the early coalfield situated well to the west – Washington, Penshaw and beyond – the construction of long waggonways from the pits to deep-water collier staiths was not feasible

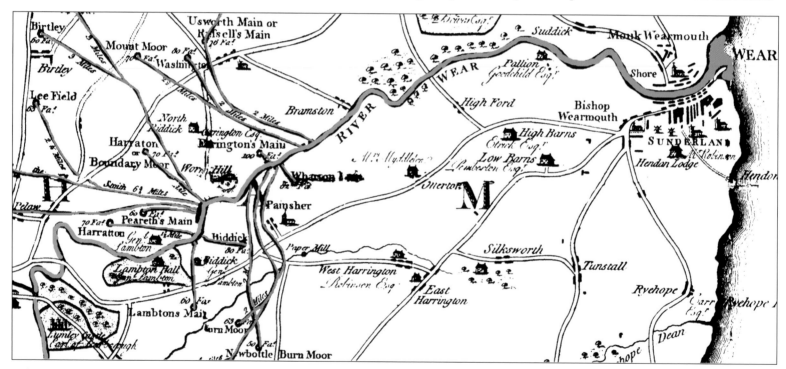

Gibson's coalfield map of 1787. These upriver staiths meant that keels had to be used to bring the coal down to the collier berths at Sunderland. The ground east of Painsher (Penshaw) was thickly capped by magnesian limestone and unexploited.

until 1812. Until then all the lines came down to the river around the Fatfield area on the north bank and Penshaw on the south, where the coal was loaded onto keels to be taken downstream to the colliers at Sunderland.

The very early history of the Wear waggonways is little understood but it centred on this short loading area on the river, unlike the miles available on the banks of the Tyne. The first line was probably the Flatts or Allan's waggonway of 1693, leading from pits north-west of Chester-le-Street down to Fatfield. By 1710 the neighbouring staiths served Dean Hedworth's waggonway to his pits around Pelton and there may have been a further line to the Washington area. On the south bank, it is likely that a waggonway was constructed about 1697 from Newbottle to staiths at Penshaw; by the 1730s there were certainly routes there from the collieries owned by the Lambton, Lumley and Tempest families.

The great expansion of mining through the eighteenth century saw a matching, and necessary, growth of the waggonway system to the river. From Fatfield staiths, the Flatts line was extended to Pelton and Hedworth's, almost parallel with it, to Beamish, with new routes added from Usworth, Birtley, Harraton and other local areas, whilst the Washington waggonway not only went down to the Wear but north to the Tyne at Pelaw. On the southern riverbank around Penshaw, the existing lines were modified and expanded – they carried heavy traffic but were not so extensive a network as that to Fatfield. Nor was the Wear system in general as large as that serving the Tyne, which, in 1800 was exporting 1.8 million tons of coal to Sunderland's 0.8 million, but, as these figures suggest, the amount was still quite massive for the period and such a tonnage could not have been transported by road.

The Penshaw routes in particular experienced the wholesale changes in waggonway working that characterised the first quarter of the nineteenth century. Here, John Buddle, 'King of the Coal Trade' was effectively managing the interests of the young 'Radical

Buddle's 'containerisation' at the Lambton berth, Sunderland. Purpose-built waggons had brought the tub containers to be loaded into keels upriver. At the harbour, a riverside steam crane transfers the coal into the ship's hold.

Jack' Lambton, owner of the great family coal royalties. In 1814, Buddle arranged for the colliery's waggonway system to be adapted for William Chapman-designed locomotives, which entailed a major reworking of the lines and their conversion to iron rails. The trial engine turned out to be ineffective and Buddle re-engineered the waggonways for stationary haulage engines and balanced planes. He also installed a system of 'containerisation' on the network, based on an idea already used on some canals, where the coal was loaded into tubs at the pit head, taken by rail down to the

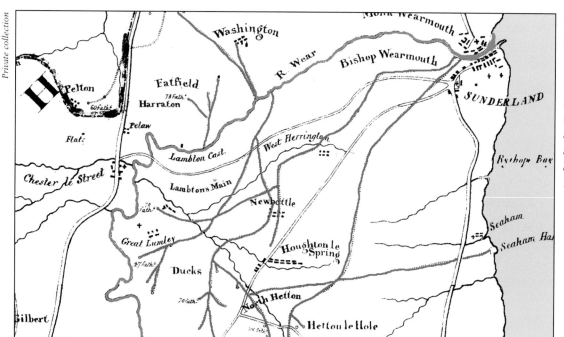

The east Durham coalfield and its waggonways (highlighted here) saw basic changes in the early nineteenth century. Londonderry has plugged his routes into his new harbour at Seaham. Lambton collieries have taken over the Newbottle line and connected it to their own system, giving direct access to Sunderland as has the Hetton colliery as it proved the coalfield beneath the limestone. From The State of the Coal Trade, *1829.*

staith then the tubs craned into specially-fitted keels to be sent down to the colliers at Sunderland, so avoiding the breakages of the coal which were the inevitable and costly result of loose reloading.

In 1812 John Douthwaite Nesham built an ambitious iron-railed line which was the first colliery waggonway to go directly to Sunderland, but it was cripplingly expensive to build and run. The route to the deep water port was intrinsically difficult, due to the ring of hills blocking the access to Wearmouth, but the advantage of a direct line, avoiding the use of keels, was obvious and would dominate the planning of future waggonways.

In 1819, Buddle relinquished his Lambton consultancy to manage the neighbouring Londonderry colliery group and here, too, he introduced the tub system, this time using an ingenious and very early floating steam crane at Sunderland for loading the colliers and again attempted to run the waggonway with locomotives. He had taken over direction of the pits from a remarkable man called Arthur Mowbray, who went on to develop the Hetton colliery and railway. Hetton was a very important pit. It was the first to be sunk through the magnesium limestone that formed a thick cap over the

Hetton Colliery, 1823

From William Hutchinson *The History and Antiquities of ... Durham*

'Hetton Colliery … at this pit Locomotive Steam Engines, or, as they are called by the coalminers, Steam Horses, each carrying 20 waggons full of coal, are used in conveying coal from the pit to the staith, a distance upwards of 7 miles, along a common waggonway … another of the wonderful improvements of the age.'

coal measures south and east of Newbottle – its success spawned the exploitation of the 'concealed coalfield' of eastern Durham. To move his coal, Mowbray commissioned George Stephenson to construct a new waggonway from Hetton over a series of hills to Sunderland. Its completion, in 1822, caused a sensation. It was, perhaps, the first railway of any length to be purpose-built for mechanical haulage, using a combination of rope-haulage with stationary engines, inclined planes and steam locomotives over an eight-mile line. The difficulties of the route, the combination of devices and the great cost of construction caused wide interest nationally and internationally, much of it centred on the use of locomotives. They had been built by Stephenson, based on his series of Killingworth engines; despite being used on only two parts of the route they were very influential on the appreciation of the locomotive as a practical source for railway power. A succession of engineers beat a path to Hetton and Killingworth to study them at work – George Stephenson had been projected into the national arena.

Ironically, it was rope haulage and the inclined plane that would form the basis of the waggonways developed to serve Sunderland. The local gradients were generally too severe for the underpowered locomotives of the day – at Hetton itself they were withdrawn from one of their two stretches of line and replaced by stationary engines. When the Lambton group bought out the Newbottle Colliery in 1822, they rearranged the waggonway to work principally by ropes, as did Buddle when he modernised the Londonderry system and built a line to the new Seaham Harbour.

The most ambitious of these non-locomotive railways – and the first passenger line to serve Sunderland – was the Durham & Sunderland Railway (D&SR). Opened in 1836, its route went from the staiths near Barrack Street down to the coast at Ryhope, inland to Murton, crossed the coalfield via Pittington and later reached to Shincliffe. It was essentially a colliery line, serving many of the pits

The incline at Copt Hill down to Hetton Dene. Despite the famous use of locomotives at Hetton Colliery, the cable inclines were used continuously from 1822 until closure.

either *en route* or with short branches, but the sets of coal waggons also had rudimentary passenger carriages attached. This formed what a railway guide described in 1842 as: 'the longest public railway in the kingdom worked entirely by the fixed-engine system, and exhibits clearly the inefficiency of this plan for passenger-traffic.' There were eight stationary steam engines working extremely long ropes, leading to 'the difficulty of starting the trains, the numerous detentions on the way, and a great uncertainty of the time that a journey will occupy, added to the jolts experienced by passengers when reaching a bank-head, or when making a false start.' Despite these chronic travelling conditions, the railway was carrying over 77,000 passengers by 1838. The line had a typically eccentric episode soon after it opened. Perhaps because traffic had

The Hetton Colliery by Thomas Hair, about 1840. Stephenson's locomotives had long been withdrawn from the mid-section of the waggonway and now worked purely from the pit head to the first incline – apparently without needing rails.

Hair's view of the winding engine at Pittington, on the Durham & Sunderland Railway, c.1840, with its strange little passenger coaches.

The Victoria Bridge under construction in 1838, above, and, below, the fine piers and arches of the completed bridge.

stopped when one of the winding drums burst under the strain (which they were rather prone to do), a waggon was fitted up with a mast and sail and merrily sped along the track at 10 mph, then succeeded in pulling a set of five more waggons.

The railway was never a financial success however and it was bought up by George Hudson in 1846 to be amalgamated into his newly-organised York & Newcastle Railway. Hudson's influence was as great on the Wearside railways as it was in Tyneside, the more so as he had been elected one of Sunderland's MPs the previous year. Already in 1844 he had scooped up the short Durham Junction line as part of his intended main line to Gateshead and

hence acquired not only a vital river crossing but certainly the most attractive Wearside rail bridge ever built.

Designed by Walker & Burges the Victoria Bridge was based on the Roman bridge at Alcantara in Spain and built with four particularly slim and elegant main arches. The engineer in charge was T.E. Harrison, originally apprenticed to William Chapman and

THE NEW RAILWAY STATION, MONKWEARMOUTH.

The newly opened Monkwearmouth Station in 1848 remains almost unchanged. It is considered one of the finest small stations in the country.

named the Victoria Bridge and became a celebrated railway structures. Unfortunately it was well over budget, and the line it served was not a financial success.

George Hudson first gained a foothold in Sunderland with the acquisition of the Brandling Junction Railway in 1844. This not only gave him routes between Gateshead and South Shields but the spur line down to Monkwearmouth, on the north bank of the river. The line had a short branch to North Dock and a rudimentary wooden terminus for passengers with plans for a permanent station, but the Brandling failed to prosper and the station was not built. Hudson resurrected the scheme in the year that he became the local MP – it was entirely in character then that he should commission a grand new station for the good of the railway and the glory of George Hudson.

The design was by local architect Thomas Moore – a neo-classical frontage with a heavily-columned portico and side wings terminating in curved pavillions. Monkwearmouth Station opened in 1848, at the height of Hudson's fame and just a year before his fall. The old wooden terminus became a freight yard; the north bank was also served by a number of short limestone waggonways direct from the quarries to the river. On the south side of the river, Hudson retained control of the Wearmouth Dock Company despite losing his other chairmanships, developing the important South Dock and improving its rail connections. In the early 1850s he built a seven-mile line, the Penshaw branch, connecting with the main line Victoria Bridge at Lambton, then going east alongside the river to Millfield and connecting with the D&SR at Hendon Junction to serve the docks. There were passenger facilities, including a station to serve Sunderland in Fawcett Street, but the line was primarily designed for freight. The Lambton collieries had their own considerable system, including the direct Newbottle line to its staiths, but increasingly rerouted their traffic to use the new Penshaw route.

later to partner Robert Stephenson in the High Level Bridge. This was one of the most ambitious rail crossings to be attempted at the time. Over 800 feet long and built almost wholly of stone from nearby Penshaw, the largest arch spanned 160 feet with a height above the river of 125 feet. The last stone was laid on the day of Queen Victoria's Coronation in 1838; in commemoration it was

The D&SR was converted from cable haulage to steam locomotives and in 1858 the old, inconvenient passenger terminus on the Town Moor was replaced by a new station at Hendon. Here and at Ryhope it had connections with the Londonderry Seaham & Sunderland Railway (LS&SR) which was, like the Lambton, privately owned. The Marquis of Londonderry not only had extensive collieries in the area but had built the town and harbour at Seaham – with his own new port already becoming clogged with colliers he determined to build a line to the South Dock at Sunderland which could carry his own and neighbouring collieries' coal. It was opened in 1854 for freight and a year later to passengers, although the arrangements were rather ramshackle at times. One manager remembered an episode from its early days when the engine broke down. Instead of the Sunderland train arriving at Seaham at 8pm, it didn't appear until nearly midnight, pulled by two horses: 'At first the passengers were indignant, but this soon gave way to laughing and funny remarks. The stops were considered as part of the play

A view of c.1900, probably showing Hall Dene Station on the privately-owned Londonderry Railway. It was taken over by the NER in 1900.

A house damaged by construction of the Southwick Railway in 1875 – compensation of £190 was awarded. Deep cuttings are often tricky, as the Sunderland Metro was to discover.

Wearmouth Railway Bridge under construction in 1879, with the Lambton staiths in the foreground. Its neighbour beyond is Robert Stephenson's rebuild of the early iron Wear road bridge, itself replaced in 1929.

and little more notice was taken of them. It was considered a great satisfaction that they got home at all.' Part of the line is now used as the coast route to Hartlepool.

By the 1870s, Wearside had a comprehensive railway system. The NER had the Brandling line with the main freight shed at Monkwearmouth, a branch to the North Dock and passenger routes to South Shields, Gateshead and Newcastle. A new line had been added three years before, the independent Hylton, Southwick & Monkwearmouth Railway serving the industry of the north bank – it was absorbed into the NER network in 1883. On the other side of the Wear, the South Dock and the Lambton and Hetton staiths were connected to the various colliery railways with passenger lines to Penshaw, Durham, Seaham and Hartlepool. As on Tyneside, there was an associated infrastructure of sidings, marshalling yards and depots together with a series of short lines to

works and shipyards. But there was a glaring gap in this network – no railway crossed the river at Sunderland itself, so there was no through route along the coast.

It was solved by building a new line from Monkwearmouth across the river, through the heart of Sunderland to link with the Hartlepool route at Ryhope. The bridge was one of the last major designs by the long-serving Engineer of the NER, T.E. Harrison, who had been involved with the Victoria and High Level Bridges so many years before. His wrought iron Wear Rail Bridge still carries the rail traffic over the river today, a bowstring girder spanning 300 feet, with the

Harrison's impressive arched roof for Sunderland Station – later to be badly damaged by a bomb in the Second World War. At the north end of the station the lines disappeared into tunnels towards Monkwearmouth Bridge, so that the platforms themselves were effectively in a roofed cutting.

ironwork supplied, as in the High Level, by Hawks of Gateshead – it was at the time the largest of its type in the world. The line through Sunderland was a problem, as the town centre was naturally heavily built-up. It became necessary to buy and demolish a string of buildings to construct a long cut-and-cover tunnel, with a brand new Central Station to serve the town. The first designs were dismissed by the local press as too mean for such a large town. The eventual building by William Bell was either a grand and fitting memorial to High Victorian architecture or a mock-gothic monstrosity, depending on the point of view. The platforms were accessed from separate north and south entrances with the train shed covered by an overall arched roof designed by Harrison.

The grand edifice of William Bell's Central Station.

Queen Alexandra Bridge under construction, 1909. Wallsend had its **Steam Elephant**, it was to turn out that the NER had a white elephant.

Sunderland's new main station opened in 1879; as a result Hendon and Fawcett Street closed, with Monkwearmouth converted from a terminus to a through station.

The town could now enjoy express rail connections with Newcastle and major cities to the south. When the NER took over the Londonderry Railway in 1900, it was already planning a coastal line to Hartlepool – its existing route was a circuitous one inland. Able now to take advantage of the Seaham line, it opened the new route five years later and further improved its services from Sunderland. At the same time, the company began construction of a bridge over the Wear between Southwick and Millfield; like the High Level at Newcastle it carried the track on top and a roadway below with Sunderland council paying part of the cost. The design was by Charles Augustus Harrison, the nephew of T.E. and comprised a lattice girder bridge on granite piers, built at great expense. As its function was to carry coal trains it was engineered on a massive scale – its great central span of 330 feet was the heaviest in Britain. The NER had expected that the bridge would ease the heavy coal traffic movements to South Dock but it became a financial disaster. The Dock experienced its highest total of coal-handling in 1904; between the start of construction of the Queen Alexandra Bridge in 1905 and completion four years later the traffic it was intended to handle had dropped considerably and would continue to fall. The upper rail deck closed in 1921, carried anti-

Staff at Sunderland Station, 1900.

Lambton staiths, once intensely busy and now a city park. The rail tunnel through a rock outcrop to the neighbouring Hetton staiths site still exists, but little more.

aircraft batteries and searchlights during the Second World War, and was finally removed in 1985. The roadway continues in use as the city's westerly river crossing.

The great coal staiths and waggonway systems of the Lambton and Hetton collieries were linked by the amalgamation of the companies in 1911, with the main depot centralised at Philadelphia. Between the wars the various local coal railways adjusted, as they always had, to the closure of old collieries and modifications to the lines. The rail network they had available allowed the use of a number of ports from the Tyne down to the Tees; the NER had a particular interest in a choice of routes as they owned Hartlepool and Tyne Docks but not Sunderland's. But like many of the old industries in the North East the collieries were hit hard during the Depression years and their strengths were failing. The passenger services, now under the LNER, remained intact with a new station serving Seaburn opened in 1937. However, proposals in 1908 and 1935 to continue the Tyneside electrification on the routes from Sunderland to Newcastle and South Shields were not carried out. Although Wearside did not suffer the same dismissal as Gateshead, the prime services were to remain firmly centred on the ECML and Newcastle.

The cutting back of the rail system experienced on Tyneside after the Second World War was to happen to Wearside but with even greater severity. In 1953 the old Durham-Sunderland line was closed. Between 1963 and 1965 the local network was hit by a succession of blows, with the closure to passengers of the Leamside line, the Penshaw branch to Durham and the services to South Shields – by 1968 the only Wearside stations still open were Sunderland Central and Seaton, with the line to Newcastle taken over by the PTE in 1974. Central itself had been badly bomb-damaged in 1940. In 1953 it was modernised, with much of the remaining roof removed and reconstructed again with new buildings twelve years later. During the 1960s and 1970s the expresses from Newcastle via Sunderland were slowly withdrawn although a new service to London was started in 1983 using the High Speed Train.

While the passenger routes were greatly reduced, the freight lines were effectively removed. They had always been centred on coal movement so that, inevitably, as the Durham collieries suffered increasing closures and became centred on the coastal strip, the old network was shut down. Stephenson's Hetton waggonway closed in 1959; the Lambton & Hetton staiths in 1967 together with their rail systems; the last of the Lambton lines in 1986. Three years earlier, South Dock was still taking 1.5 million tons of coal a year, mainly for shipping to power stations, but by the early 1990s most of this traffic was

The Romance of Steam – Sunderland in 1959. Cuttings through town centres were liable to cover them in smoke and grit.

Hetton-le-Hole station in c.1905, left, and c.1960, right.

The NCB took over a very extensive network of colliery lines. Here, their engine No. 55 with a coal train from North Moor to Lambton staiths.

being redirected to Tyne Dock. Now the Durham collieries and the complex of Wearside coal railways have gone completely, as have nearly all the freight lines in the area. South Dock is a shadow of its former self, North Dock has been reduced to a yacht marina. All the shipyards have gone, together with their internal rail systems as have most of the older industries strung along the freight routes that followed the north and south banks of the river. As on Tyneside, their whole infrastructure of marshalling yards, sidings, goods yards and level crossings has gone with them.

Sunderland starts the twenty-first century with a rail system barely adequate for a city. There are regional services to Teesside and Newcastle and direct services on the trans-Pennine route to Liverpool via York, Manchester and Leeds, but none to London and the south.

The most significant development in the recent history of Wearside's railways is the long-awaited link to the Metro. Opened by the Queen during her Golden Jubilee tour in 2002, the line from Sunderland Station to South Hylton uses the old Pallion line, although a total rebuilding was necessary. The route to Newcastle is shared, uniquely in Britain between the Metro and the traditional railway.

Three of the Doxford shipyard engines in steam. The company had a total of four steam cranes and all were preserved – **Hendon** *is at Tanfield Railway. The industry was not so fortunate; shipbuilding on the Wear has disappeared as have virtually all the company and colliery railways.*

Sunderland Station, December 1952, during the removal of the bomb-damaged roof. The entire station was demolished and rebuilt in 1965.

The NER crossing a lane near Sunderland at the beginning of the twentieth century. This casual yet intimate relationship with the railway, so typical of Tyne and Wear, is now a distant memory.

The Legacy of the Railways

Ian Ayris

It may seem strange to write of the legacy of the railways when they remain a fundamental part of our everyday lives. There is undoubtedly a heritage and an archaeology of our industrial past – of the coal industry, of the iron and steel industry, (which whilst clinging ever more desperately to life are, within our region at least, things of the increasingly distant past) and of the railways. Indeed railway museums and the fantastically active railway preservation movement have largely focused on that key element of the development of the railways which has been lost – steam. But a legacy, unlike heritage and archaeology, is not only about what once was lost and now is found, but is about elements of the past which are relevant today and will continue to influence the future.

The railways were at the heart of the nineteenth and twentieth century industrial and transport matrix which shaped the nation – they were instrumental in forging communities, landscapes and societies. Railways fostered the development of suburbs and satellite towns, connecting them with major towns and cities and then linking those major towns and cities with each other – uniting the United Kingdom. The adoption of standard railway time across the country brought not only unity but uniformity in time as well as space. The sheer pace of travel drew the country together. Britain became

The working replicas of the **Steam Elephant** and **Locomotion** at the Pockerley waggonway, Beamish. The Museum attracts some 300,000 visitors a year.

Andy Guy

NEWCASTLE CENTRAL RAILWAY STATION

This plaque celebrates the 150th anniversary of the station, opened by Queen Victoria on 29th August 1850 and built by the York, Newcastle and Berwick Railway. It was designed by John Dobson, Architect and Robert Stephenson, Engineer. The portico on the north facade, designed by Thomas Prosser, Architect, was added by the North Eastern Railway in 1860. The train shed roof was extended southwards in 1893 to the design of William Bell, Architect.

The building is listed Grade I.

a smaller place, an accessible place with a common currency of not just tracks, stations and signal boxes but also tickets, timetables and clocks. Only the remotest parts of the kingdom remained untouched. Whilst not undermining regional identity the railways were fundamental in fostering the national cohesion which in times of peril (war) and rejoicing (Golden Jubilees and World Cups) is still recognisable today. Landscape, time, and national identity are mighty big concepts to lay at the door of what is, after all, merely a means of getting from A to B. But if you accept that the role of the railway has largely been superseded by that of the motorway, the dual carriageway and the trunk road and then consider the contribution, for good or bad, that the post-war road infrastructure has made to the appearance of the country, to its economic growth and to our daily lives and you begin to understand the role and signifi-

cance the railways previously had in shaping the country. The railway legacy is a deep-seated legacy but also one with a strong physical manifestation.

In the North East where regeneration and reclamation have swept away much of the region's industrial history, the heritage of the railways is probably now the area's strongest link with its industrial past. The transport routes and the engineering achievements which followed in the wake of, and grew with the burgeoning coal industry, are still an intrinsic part of the landscape. Many remarkable nineteenth century bridges survive and are still in use, the routes of eighteenth and nineteenth century waggonways and railways have survived in parts of Tyne and Wear where neither urban expansion nor opencast mining has disturbed the landscape. Indeed, some surviving aspects of the region's heritage of Victorian railway expansion are of *national* significance. The factors which have determined the survival of sites have been diverse: continued use in the modern rail system; adaptive reuse of buildings and routes; the work of preservation societies and museums; protection through the 'listing' of buildings and the 'scheduling' of monuments; and serendipity – the happy survival of buildings, machines, structures, earthworks and artefacts which have largely escaped man's predilection to interfere.

Railway preservation groups have been at the forefront of the move to celebrate and animate the heritage of the country's industrial and transport history. From the beginnings of the movement in 1950, which saw the preservation of Britain's first 'heritage' railway – the Talyllyn Railway in Mid Wales – there are now over 100 preserved railways across Great Britain, using close to 500 miles of track and 570 station buildings . They are the embodiment of volunteer activity in the country's heritage and are an invaluable tourist resource – by 1999 the turnover from preserved railways was in the region of £43m. In the main they capture a sense of style, evoke the era of steam, often pass through the greenest of

England's green and pleasant land and preserve examples of a bewildering array of locomotives with unfathomable variations in age, type and size. They do not however in most cases preserve the long history of the railways or of their built heritage. Less than a quarter of the preserved railways in the country contain buildings or structures which are seen as important enough to be listed buildings or scheduled monuments. Happily Tyne and Wear bucks this trend. The Bowes, preserved by the Bowes Railway Company, is the only railway in the country which is, throughout its preserved length, a Scheduled Ancient Monument – placing it, in theory at least, among the nation's most prestigious protected sites along with Stone Henge, Ironbridge Gorge and the like. The Tanfield Railway contains a mid-Victorian engine shed and has, as a nearby neighbour, Causey (or Tanfield) Arch – arguably the world's oldest railway bridge. In the Victoria Tunnel, the mile-and-a-half long early Victorian subterranean colliery waggonway route which runs under the streets of Newcastle, the region has a quite remarkable survival of both its mining and railway past. The Robert Stephenson Trust have achieved the preservation of one of the country's most important railway-related buildings – part of the former Robert Stephenson Works in South Street, Newcastle, the world's first purpose-built locomotive factory.

The role of statutory protection has been fundamental to the retention of many of the area's most important railway buildings, and in ensuring that the fundamental character and appearance of many others has been retained. The protection given by 'listing' has been highly instrumental in guarding buildings such as the Stephenson Works and parts of the Greenesfield Engine Works in Gateshead from demolition. A host of the region's most important railway buildings are thus protected: Newcastle's Central Station, which carries the highly prestigious Grade I listing; the former Jesmond Railway

Tanfield Railway, August Bank Holiday 2002. The working displays here, at the Bowes Railway and at Beamish vividly bring to life the excitement – and variety – of the railway age.

Greenesfield in 2002, derelict and awaiting redevelopment.

A new mosaic at Whitley Bay brings a splash of colour to the Edwardian station.

Station, a fine Tudor style Victorian suburban station; Dial Cottage, the former home of George Stephenson; Tynemouth Station, a delightful example of an elegant English seaside Station; Whitley Bay, West Monkseaton and South Shields stations, functioning parts of the contemporary Metro system; and Monkwearmouth Station, now a dedicated railway museum under the aegis of Tyne and Wear Museums and considered one of the finest small monumental station buildings in the country. The listings extend to an array of impressive bridges. In the heyday of the railways there were thought to be 2.5 bridges for every mile of track, making them the most common of all rail related structures. Led by the Newcastle-Gateshead High Level Bridge and the Victoria Viaduct at Washington, both of which are of national significance, there are numerous listed railway bridges across the region – King Edward VII Bridge and Scotswood Rail Bridge over the Tyne, the Ouseburn and Willington Viaducts of the former Newcastle and North Shields Railway and the Queen Alexandra and Wearmouth Railway Bridges over the River Wear.

But this is only to deal with iconic structures. Stations were indeed a significant product of the development of passenger railways. Before the railways brought the ability to carry passengers in great numbers there had been no need for a specific building for travellers to congregate. Stations portrayed and exemplified the prestige and importance of the railways but they were only one amongst a range of buildings required for running them. Many types of structure were lost with the end of the steam age – the typical raised water tanks for example. The reduction of the system and the closure of most branch lines reduced the need for many signal boxes and pieces of way side equipment, further reducing the number of surviving features from the railways of old. Proposals to rapidly assess the survival of these and many other aspects of the industry in England at least, under English Heritage's Monuments Protection Plan await implementation but in this case, in a wholly inappropriate metaphor, the horse has surely bolted.

Where the heritage of the railways in Tyne and Wear does survive most impressively however is, fittingly, in its routes. The enormous significance of the Tyneside area in the early development of the waggonway and of the locomotive was founded on the movement of coal. The extensive colliery waggonway system, rather than the later Victorian passenger railway network, forms one of the key elements of the area's rail heritage. Local Authorities and SUSTRANS have developed a series of footpaths, cycleways and bridleways on the former trackbeds of the region. The reuse of former railway lines in this way is a national phenomenon and not specific to the North East, however the significant difference here is that many of the Tyne and Wear lines hold particular importance in the history of the railway. Benjamin Thompson's Brunton and Shields Railway, the eighteenth century Tanfield Railway and Wylam Waggonway, the pioneering Stephenson lines of the Bowes and Hetton Railways and Lord Londonderry's ambitious line to his newly built Seaham Harbour are all now wholly or in part public rights of way. A site of little known but particular significance for example lies beneath the feet of walkers on Walbottle Moors where the earthworks of the late eighteenth century Walbottle Moors Waggonway, which unlike many similar routes, was never overlain

Andy Guy

Lintz Green Station on the railway line to Consett and now part of the Derwent Valley Walk. The transport revolution seems to have come round full circle.

by a later nineteenth century railway, can still be traced. The preservation of these routes for contemporary leisure use is now combined with the exploitation of their archaeological potential to better understand their historic development. Archaeological excavation of the wooden waggonway at Lambton D Pit was a breakthrough in our appreciation of how horse drawn waggonways were constructed at the end of the eighteenth century. Further work on the pioneering line of the Bowes Railway has taken that story on to

A cartoon from the Illustrated London News, 1846, *lamenting the destruction wreaked by the railways.*

Metro system; some of the very earliest waggonway routes are travelled daily; important sites and buildings are protected by listing and preserved through continued or adaptive re-use. The microcosm of railway history contained within an area which encircles Newcastle Central Station, the High Level Bridge, the former Robert Stephenson and Hawthorn Engineering Works, the King Edward VII Bridge and the Greenesfield Engine Works would be difficult to match for significance any where in the world. But in creating a part of that remarkable series of structures our forefathers laid waste to an earlier heritage – the railway was taken directly through the site of the city's historic castle (see frontispiece). Even in the late 1840s heritage and progress did not always make comfortable bedfellows. The role of our heritage as part of the nation's culture and in the regeneration of the economy is, however,

the beginning of the locomotive era. This type of work is vital in safeguarding the future of the railway heritage. Indeed, understanding buildings and structures is now seen as the basis for conservation of all aspects of our historic environment. Unfolding research work on the important surviving buildings of Robert Stephenson's Works, for example, will underpin the conservation of what will be a key site in the exceptional railway heritage of Tyne and Wear.

The legacy of the railways within Newcastle and throughout Tyne and Wear is highly visible – its heritage is in use today. Newcastle Central Station is still one of the country's principle stations as well as one of its finest; historic stations form part of the

now much better understood. A similar fate should not await the surviving railway heritage. For the story of the railways is one which brings together both heritage and progress; it is a story of continuity – with a past, a present and a future. It is a journey which is far from over.

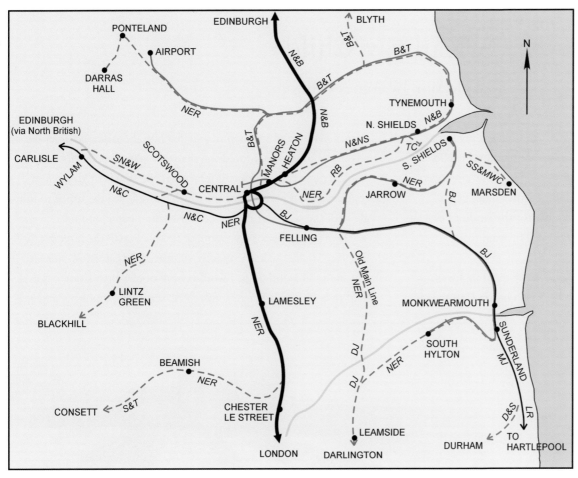

Tony Liddell

The passenger lines of Tyne and Wear between 1850 and the present day.

N

KEY

Metro Line

East Coast Mainline

Open Today

Closed Since 1920

B&T	Blyth & Tyne
BJ	Brandling Junction
D&S	Durham & Sunderland
DJ	Durham Junction
LR	Londonderry
MJ	Monkwearmouth Junction (LNER)
N&B	Newcastle & Berwick
N&DJ	Newcastle & Darlington Junction

N&C	Newcastle & Carlisle
N&NS	Newcastle and North Shields
NER	North Eastern Railway
RB	Riverside Branch
S&T	Stanhope & Tyne
SN&W	Scotswood, Newburn & Wylam
SS&MWC	South Shields, Marsden & Whitburn
TC	Tyne Commission Quay (NER)

A Railway Child

Recollection by Agnes Chilton

I was destined to become a railway child the moment my father met my mother on the platform of Lamesley station. Invalided out of the army towards the end of World War I, his employers sent him to resume his railway career in the relative quiet of a country station. My mother was the daughter of the landlord of the Ravensworth Arms, and she often travelled by train from Lamesley to Gateshead or Newcastle.

They married two years later in 1924, and by the time I was born my father had been transferred to the much busier Gateshead station. Mum and I sometimes visited him there during quiet periods in the timetable. I loved the shadowy station under its densely smoked glass roof. I can still remember the smells of steam and coal tar, mixed with engine oil which wafted into the office to mingle with the scents of carbolic soap, carbon paper and ink.

Dad's office was cosy from the fire blazing in the large black fireplace where the kettle quietly simmered. My greatest pleasure was his solid wood desk. I would climb onto a high stool and pretend to be a post office or bank clerk, scribbling on forms and rub-

Lamesley Station c.1920.

Gateshead East Station in the 1950s.

ber-stamping them in red or black ink while the clock ticked seriously on the wall.

Gateshead was a bustling station. Many shipyard and industrial workers travelled from there to their jobs on the Tyne and in Sunderland. It was exciting to hear the express trains rushing through the station, heralded by a loud bang as they entered, and ending with a swish then silence. Smaller local trains made grinding, squealing noises as they drew to a halt. You would hear porters calling the name of the station followed by the rhythmic slamming of carriage doors. As the guard's shrill whistle signalled it was safe, the great iron horse went on its way with a powerful snort of steam and an arrogant toot.

After about two years, Dad moved to Newcastle Central Station where he spent the rest of his career. It was an even more exhilarating place. Because of his increased responsibility, regular visits to his office became a thing of the past. I did once have a tour of the underground control room, where Dad and his colleagues used radar to control the movement of rolling stock. We also visit-

ed on special occasions. In the late 1940s, I remember watching a military parade from his office which was situated above the main portico. I also remember the excited crowds gathering at the Central Station to meet film and theatre stars who were visiting the North East. Hollywood idols received an especially rapturous reception. I particularly remember the visit of Eddy Cantor, my father's favourite film comedian, because Dad made sure he was part of the official reception.

Saturday was Dad's half day. My mother and I would spend the morning shopping, then visit the ladies' rest room at the Central Station. It was a very select place for travellers to wait. There was a brightly burning fire, easy chairs and even a writing desk. Toilet facilities in the adjoining room were solid and Victorian. They were very well kept by a severe looking attendant who sat at the door of her 'office', guarding her piles of clean towels (wash and brush up twopence), hard, shiny toilet rolls and first aid kit. There were always columns of pennies which the attendant grudgingly exchanged for silver if a customer needed change for the facilities. Most larger stations had similar WCs, all reeking of Jeyes fluid, and all presided over by identical battleaxes. There were also general waiting rooms in stations, but they were quite bare and dingy with wooden seats around the walls. Their toilets were always clean, but less well appointed.

Mum and I would meet Dad near Smith's bookstall where I bought *Sunny Stories* and later *Girls' Crystal*. Sometimes we'd have a sandwich and a cup of tea in the station buffet. They were busy all the time, noisy, smoky, steamy and warm. Tea, coffee, cocoa, Bovril, Oxo and alcoholic drinks were served over a high wooden counter. Rock buns were displayed in large glass jars, sandwiches were cut to order.

As a Saturday treat we occasionally had lunch in the more elegant station restaurant with waiter service and excellent food. Railway hotels, like Newcastle's Station Hotel, were deservedly

Newcastle Central Station in 1938.

considered high class.

First and third class travel were vastly different. I wonder if the absence of a second class was designed to reinforce class differences?

Third class wasn't at all uncomfortable, but it was certainly austere, with lino flooring and upholstered bench seating. The seating was intended to accommodate as many people as possible, but later armrests were added to divide the compartment into eight seats. By contrast, first class had luxurious colour co-ordinated carpets and curtains, well upholstered seat cushions, with only six seats per compartment, and walls clad in highly polished wood.

There were similar differences in overnight sleepers. Third class consisted of four bunk compartments, strictly segregated into male

or female only. You slept in close proximity to strangers. Each traveller was provided with two pillows and a rug. The WC was along the corridor. First class sleepers had double or single compartments, with comfortable one-tier beds, fine linen bedding, thick woollen blankets, monogrammed coverlets and a chamber pot in a cupboard under the window. Singles had small washbasins. Morning tea was available in both classes. I remember being woken up by a firm shake on my shoulder as a tray was offered to me and a strong, deep voice warned 'Very hot, very heavy'.

Dealing with luggage was simple. When you bought your return ticket, you could pay a little extra, and a carrier would pick up your luggage from home and deliver it to your destination. On your return journey the process would be reversed. You never had to carry a case if you didn't want to. If you wanted to take your luggage on the train, there were always plenty of porters to help. Most, though not all, people tipped them for this service. Porters weren't paid much and tips gave a much-needed boost to their income.

During World War II, when I was in my early teens, my parents allowed me to visit a cousin in London. I spent a week there during a short lull in the relentless bombing of the city. Railway travel during war time was much more stressful. Trains were packed to capacity, and there was no guarantee of a seat, no matter how long the journey.

Members of the armed forces were constantly on the move,

either going home on leave or returning to duty. Many would have no idea of their ultimate destination, as they rejoined units which could be sent to theatres of war anywhere in the world. Nurses, munitions workers, land girls, firemen and civil servants were also moved about the country, according to the demands of the war. Then there were ordinary people; mothers visiting evacuated children, or wives and girlfriends travelling to snatch a few precious hours with a partner.

In war time, no one paid much attention to the normal eight bodies per compartment rule. If you could squeeze into a seat, you did. If not, you stood in a crowded corridor, or sat on your case, much to the annoyance of anyone trying to walk through the train. Suddenly it became acceptable for servicemen to sit while ladies stood. Everyone was

Central Station c.1936, with Jubilee train.

conscious that each exhausted-looking man could have just disembarked from a ship that had been battling at sea for months on end, or had endured endless flying hours over enemy territory, or had been under constant bombardment on a distant battlefield.

It was strange to be one of the crowd in a dimly-lit train passing through eerie, blacked-out stations. On my journey to London, I was lucky enough to find a seat, but I still had a very uncomfortable ride. Passengers were standing in the compartments as well as in the corridors, and one woman sat on her case which was pushed against my leg so I couldn't move.

Wartime stations were places of high drama. There were always tearful farewells and joyous re-unions. You would see small wedding parties escorting the bride and groom to the station. One,

or sometimes both, of the happy couple would be in uniform, returning to the war just a few hours after the ceremony. Sometimes ambulances would drive onto the platform and pull up right beside the train to receive the wounded. I suppose this not only ensured privacy for the servicemen, but also protected civilian morale from the sight of the dreadful damage that war can do.

Due to the Extreme Weather ...

One of the advantages of the early waggonways were their greater tolerance of bad weather compared to the roads of the time. Modern railways can usually handle fog, snow and light flooding better than motor traffic, but following the cut-back of the routes it can be difficult to find an alternative route when things really go wrong. If the East Coast Main Line is blocked between Newcastle and Edinburgh, for example, the only diversion is via Carlisle.

But no system is or was immune, as may be seen in the account of the blizzards of 1740 (page 11). With the development of the railways and the introduction of locomotives the problems could get worse. Points would freeze, engines loose adhesion, signals jam and nowadays the overhead electric cables are particularly vulnerable to strong winds. In 1836, Thomas Wardropper of Robert Stephenson's took out to Russia a locomotive for their first steam railway. He told the engineer of the line that, "...all the world knew that locomotive engines could travel in England in fine weather, but we wanted to prove to Russians that they could travel in Russia and in bad weather, and as we were commencing a new era in locomotives...and did not like to be beaten with trifles, such as a cold day or a handful of snow."

Ironically the Russians soon learnt to battle through their own much severer winters whilst we still suffer from 'the wrong kind of snow'. There are many accounts of local trains stuck in deep drifts, sometimes for days. Routes such as those over the Pennines were particularly vulnerable and were at the forefront in looking for solutions. In the same year that Wardropper was in Russia the

Ken Hoole Collection

January 1945, snow at Central Station making wartime conditions even chillier. The defrosted points show up clearly.

Newcastle & Carlisle fitted brooms to the front of an engine to sweep the snow off the rails and by 1842 all its locomotives had ploughs. In 1838 it was the first railway to try a sanding apparatus to improve traction. But really heavy snow could bring all the lines to a halt. As early as 1846 Newcastle was cut off by rail, despite the attempts of over 200 men to clear the line to Darlington alone and the same happened in the hard winter of 1941.

Andy Guy – NRM

The Percy Main snowplough on display at the NRM.

GREAT SNOWSTORM
IN THE
NORTH.

COMPLETE BLOCK ON THE NORTH LINE.

TWELVE TRAINS SNOWED UP.

ADVENTURES OF PASSENGERS.

Headlines in the Newcastle Weekly Chronicle *6 March 1886.*

One of the severest snowstorms was in the winter of 1886 when heavy snow was blown into deep drifts throughout the north east. As the Newcastle Weekly Chronicle reported, the snow came up beyond the carriage windows, two goods trains were 'completely buried' and at Fulwell cutting 'the drift was 12 to 16 feet deep'. For a time the area was effectively cut off by and it is a measure of the role of the railway as the main overland transport that the effects of this were numerous and serious. One train from Glasgow to Newcastle was stuck from the Tuesday morning until a rescue engine arrived late on Wednesday. Before the days of carriage heat-ing the passengers were bitterly cold but at least water was available 'by opening the foot-warmers and drinking the contents'. As for food, 'a search rewarded us with a large box of herrings' together with 'a few delicacies not forgetting half a gallon of whiskey'. The fish, which they would come to hate, were cooked on the engine shovel, 'and four rabbits, which we traced in the snow, were converted into stew by the cook of the Pulman car'.

At least the passengers could attempt to look after themselves. Elsewhere, four cattle trains with 90 trucks were caught in the drifts. 'There was no immediate prospect of these trains being released, and it was feared that many of the animals would perish from the effects of cold and hunger.' The cattle market at Newcastle was at a standstill, the mail and newspapers delayed, collieries laid off as the coal could not be moved and thousands of passengers milled around the stations waiting to see if they could get home.

Prodigious efforts were made by the railways to get the lines reopened. Powerful relief engines were sent out to try to force a passage but were becoming stuck themselves. At Cramlington, for example, 'the snow plough and 2 locomotives had become buried

Snow at Cullercoats in 1886.

Londonderry Railway and even the boys of the Netherton Reformatory sent out with shovels. It was the 1740 situation all over again, but now much more than coal was at risk.

Severe flooding tended to be confined to fairly predictable areas of particular routes. Cullercoats Station was particularly severely hit in 1900 when a train derailed in deep water outside the station. Local fishermen brought out their boats to rescue the passengers – at a price. It suffered badly again in 1903 and the 1930s, whilst, down the line, Jesmond flooded out in 1913. It has not always been a lesson well learnt – the low-lying Metro station at Newcastle Airport has had similar problems since its opening in 1991.

beneath the snow'. Here 50 men tried to dig them out. At neighbouring Killingworth, 350 men were shovelling out the drifts, 100 of them local pitmen, the others sent out from Newcastle where 'Central Station was fairly beseiged by shovel-bearing labourers eager to be employed'. It was a pattern repeated elsewhere, with over 700 men working further north, 500 attempting to clear the

Cullercoats was doubly unlucky. The station was flooded out in 1900, a train derailed, and its passengers rescued by local boatmen.

A train approaches a flooded Jesmond Station from the north, 1913.

Afterword

The development of the modern railway was one of the great landmarks in the shaping of today's world. It was fundamental in the evolution from the industrialised locality into the industrialised nation, the so-called 'Revolution' that still essentially divides the globe between the 'developed' and, that optimistic phrase, the 'developing' world.

GEORGE STEPHENSON, ENGINEER, INVENTOR OF THE LOCOMOTIVE ENGINE LIVED IN THIS COTTAGE FROM 1805 TO 1823; HIS FIRST LOCOMOTIVE (BLUCHER) WAS BUILT AT THE ADJACENT COLLIERY WAGON SHOPS, AND ON JULY 25TH 1814 WAS PLACED ON THE WAGONWAY WHICH CROSSES THE ROAD AT THE EAST END OF THIS COTTAGE.

The legend of the Stephensons. The sun dial that George and Robert carved in 1816 for their Killingworth home, with a plaque claiming George was the 'Inventor of the Locomotive Engine'. He was not — such misinformation only does a disservice to the other great local pioneers.

The North East was the cradle of the modern railway and its two essential components – an effective locomotive and a reliable iron rail. For 200 years, the colliery railways that served the two rivers grew into the greatest complex of lines to be found anywhere, then acted as the core of the mechanisation that has characterised the last 200 years. They became the model from which mainland Europe and America would develop their own rail systems, and by which Britain would be enabled to lead the World in the scale of its industrialisation.

The monuments to this great age lie everywhere in the landscape of the area. The waggonway routes from colliery to staith have at times survived as pathways or road alignments – more often they are no more than ghost images in the land. As some of the most important relics of the Industrial Revolution they deserve more careful preservation and greater efforts at presentation than they usually receive. In particular, the unique and remarkable survival of the Lambton D wooden waggonway should be recognised as one of the nation's more valuable historic sights, yet its future remains uncertain and its significance underappreciated. The greatest and grandest representative of the early waggonway age is undoubtedly Tanfield Arch and embankment – preserved, restored, well presented but unaccountably little visited.

Steam traction, the enabler of the modern railway, was developed by Tynesiders. Blenkinsop and Murray have no memorial in their home area; Buddle and Chapman's contribution has been largely forgotten. George and Robert Stephenson have not, of course – they remain perhaps the best known 'Geordies' in the

Wylam Dilly *on display in the Royal Museum of Scotland, Edinburgh.*

world. George created his most important locomotive developments at Dial Cottage, Killingworth and Robert spent his formative years there. It was the only surviving house that they shared, personalised by the sundial they together prepared, historically more significant than the famous Wylam birthplace cottage, but long closed to the public and with an undecided future.

All seven of the oldest surviving complete locomotives were built by North Easterners. *Puffing Billy* and *Rocket* can be seen in London's Science Museum, *Sans Pareil* and *Agenoria* at The National Railway Museum in York, and *Locomotion* at Darlington. *Wylam Dilly* is, by a historical quirk, entombed in the Royal Scottish Museum in Edinburgh, without context or relevance. If a fraction of the effort put into reclaiming the Lindisfarne Gospels had been put instead into the return of this local 'icon' then it

might now be in Newcastle's Discovery Museum today, sharing pride of place with *Turbinia*. But the city already has an important relic in George Stephenson's locomotive *Billy*, currently shown in Middle Engine Lane, little studied and largely unknown both within and without the area. It may be that its old resting place in Central Station in Newcastle would best make it a familiar object again.

The Bowes Railway is the only working standard gauge cable-haulage railway in the country; the preserved Tanfield Railway is not only the oldest working line in the world but has an excellent stable of locally-built locomotives. At Beamish, the Pockerley Waggonway runs replicas of *Locomotion* and the remarkable *Steam Elephant*, carrying passengers most days of the year to give a unique experience of the pioneering era and with further developments to come. The relics and treasures that the area contains are not restricted to individual objects. The record offices of Northumberland, Durham and Tyne and Wear and the library at Beamish contain many of the prime documents of the early railway and its evolution into the modern. Newcastle and Sunderland museums, libraries and art galleries have outstanding collections on this crucial process.

These are only the more obvious reminders of the role played by the railway. For anyone interested in their local history, it would be hard to find an area of Tyneside or Wearside that was more than a mile from a waggonway or railway at some time – the history of their lines and the part played in the locality often remains to be properly understood. The intensity, the all-pervading presence of the railway, is fast becoming a distant memory.

The modern railway was developed in Tyne and Wear and in its turn that railway played a crucial part in developing the region. Rail as the prime mover of people and freight has become much diminished in the last 50 years, a part of the everyday landscape that has perhaps gone forever. But still the ECML remains the best connection between London and Tyneside, the Metro the easiest way to move around its centres.

For the first time in decades the local rail system is expanding rather than contracting. The Orpheus Project is an ambitious plan by the Metro to add 100 km of new routes, including lines to Blaydon and Newburn to serve west Tyneside, Team Valley and Chowdene to the south and major extensions to the Wearside routes to include Washington and Ryhope. Some of these may well begin with buses and trams and completion of the project is not expected until 2015 but it will give greatly improved access to the light rail system for most of Tyne and Wear.

With regard to the 'traditional' railway, the old Leamside line across the Victoria Bridge is expected to open to regular traffic again, possibly with a new station at Washington. The route from Newcastle to Ashington may be restored and there are plans to improve the service between Newcastle, Sunderland and Middlesbrough with perhaps three new stations on the coast. But these remain proposals and the recent experience of major upgrades for the ECML have shown an all-too familiar pattern of promises followed by 'postponements'. The railway is still recognised as a basic part of the region's transport system as well as an essential link to the rest of the country. It is encouraging that these schemes are in response to rising passenger and freight demand – demand, that is, for a service that is reliable and affordable. The North East has a history of rail use that spans some 400 years. Its waggonways played a major role in shaping the region; the modern railway that it spawned became in turn a fun-

damental component in the creation of an industrialised world. The basic rules developed here can still be seen in the most advanced of today's railways. George Stephenson would recognise the French TGV or Japan's 'Bullet Train' as locomotive-powered systems built to his 'Killingworth' gauge; Michael Longridge would find familiar their rolled-metal edge-rails tied to a track bed. Cable haulage, vacuum power, magnetic levitation, plate rails, monorails do not form the basis of modern railways – the design principles of the Georgian North East do. There is no better place to appreciate that achievement than in the small area around the rivers Tyne and Wear.

Andy Guy

The old and the new. A freight train crosses the mainline Ouseburn Viaduct, alongside a Metro on the Byker Viaduct.

Gazetteer of Railway Sites

The surviving monuments of the railway are scattered throughout Tyne and Wear, some more obvious than others and many still in use. This is by no means a comprehensive gazetteer to the sites of interest, but an informal guide. There are now many pamphlets available in local libraries that give further information and reprints of early Ordnance Survey maps are easy to obtain, giving some idea of the tremendous extent and complexity of the railway system that once operated in the area. (CL: closed to the public – Ordnance Survey, Landranger Map 88, grid reference, NZ......)

NORTH TYNESIDE

Dial Cottage, Killingworth (CL-275705): home to George and Robert Stephenson, 1805-23. Whitley Bay Station (Metro-357719): 1910, striking free baroque style. Tynemouth Station (Metro-366693): 1882, a riot of Victorian ironwork, NER tile map. Old Tynemouth Station, Oxford Street (CL-365690): 1847, 'railway Jacobean'. Willington Viaduct (Metro-333672): 1839, still hugely impressive. Park Road, Wallsend (302666): colliery waggonway route of *Steam Elephant*.

The Willington Viaduct (from the Metro).

NEWCASTLE

Byker Viaduct (Metro-262646): 1980, modern curved bridge in concrete. Ouseburn Viaduct (ECML-264647): 1839, pair to Willington. Jesmond Station (254653): 1864, 'Tudor' red brick. Manors East Station (CL-253642): 1887, unusual curved entrance building. Manor Chare Viaduct (ECML-252642): 1848, under-regarded series of grand stone arches. The Side Viaduct (ECML-251640): 1848, spectacular single great arch. St Andrew's Church, Newgate Street (246644): monument to William Chapman. Stephenson Monument, Neville Street (247639): 1862, stranded among road traffic. Royal Station Hotel, Neville Street (247639): 1892, grand interior. Central Station (rail, Metro-246637): 1850, finest station in Britain, 1893 tiled buffet. Robert Stephenson's works, South Street (part CL, part builders merchant-247636):1823, first factory intended for locomotive building. Hawthorns works,

Manors Station

South Street

150

The Queen Elizabeth and King Edward Bridges.

Forth Street (CL-246637). Forth Street Goods, Pottery Lane (CL-246636): small concrete warehouse c.1906 survives. Newcastle & Carlisle Viaduct (CL-244635): 1847, early approach to Central. Benwell Church (218642): monument to John Buddle. Newburn Church (167654): monuments to Hedley and Hawthorn families.

TYNE BRIDGES

High Level (rail-251636):1849, Stephenson & Harrison masterpiece. Queen Elizabeth (Metro-248634): 1980, modern, steel, dignified. King Edward VII (rail-247633): 1906, workmanlike on a grand scale. Scotswood (CL-197638): 1871, series of small wrought-iron hog-backs.

GATESHEAD

Derwent Valley Walk (180599): on 1867 NER Consett line, crossing Lockhaugh Viaduct. Tyne Marshalling Yard (CL-257577): 1963, active large freight yard. Dunston Staiths (235627): 1893, timber coal staiths. Greenesfield (CL-254635): 1844, remains of old station hotel and workshops. Oakwellgate (255637): 1839, sta-

Felling Station

tion mound, staiths incorporated in new Sage music centre. Felling Station (CL-276622): 1842, tiny Brandling Junction station, oldest surviving in Tyne & Wear.

SOUTH TYNESIDE

Tyne Dock (CL-352656): 1859, much reduced NER complex. Marsden Rattler pub (400651): modern, on trackbed, clock tower and fittings from old Manors Station, carriages.

NORTHUMBERLAND

Wylam Station (N'land, rail-120645): c.1838, early station, iron footbridge and signal box.

DURHAM

Tanfield, or Causey Arch & embankment (Durham, 201559): 1727, greatest monument to waggonway age.

Wylam Station.

SUNDERLAND

Monkwearmouth Station (396577): 1848, fine classical station (see Museums). Wearmouth Railway Bridge (Metro, rail – 396574): 1879, large wrought-iron bow string. Lambton Staiths (392574): 1812, fragments remain in park, short railway tunnel. Queen Alexandra Bridge (382578): 1909, great steel girder

Queen Alexandra Bridge

bridge (heaviest span in Britain at time), roadway still used. Victoria Bridge (CL-320543): 1838, then largest span in Europe, elegant Roman design. Sustrans 'Coast to Coast' cycleway (Irish Sea-North Sea): routed mainly on old trackbed in Durham & Wearside. Lambton D (CL-318510): major wood waggonway excavation (now covered). Hetton-le-Hole Church (353474): monument to Nicholas Wood.

MUSEUMS & PRESERVED RAILWAYS

George Stephenson's cottage, Wylam (N'land, 126650): National Trust, birthplace (1781), alongside Wylam waggonway, displays. Wylam Library (N'land, 085638): small but interesting displays of historic local railway. Stephenson Railway Museum (322692): Tyne & Wear Museums, Stephenson's *Billy*, Harton Colliery and Tyneside loop electrics, industrial steam locomotives, passenger-carrying, displays. Bowes Railway (286590): only remaining working standard gauge cable-hauled railway (1826), industrial engines, displays.

Bowes Railway

Bowes Railway.

Tanfield Railway (206563): oldest working railway in world (1725), passenger-carrying, local industrial locomotives and stock, shed and yard displays. The North of England Open Air Museum, Beamish (Durham – 219542): passenger-carrying replicas of *Locomotion* and *Steam Elephant*, 1825 period displays, 1913 period colliery railway, NER railway, station, engines and rolling stock. Monkwearmouth Station (396577): Tyne & Wear Museums, booking office, Hudson portrait, displays.

FURTHER AFIELD

Darlington Railway Museum (North Road, Darlington, Durham): original *Locomotion* (1825), *Derwent* (1845), two handsome NER locomotives, extensive displays. Timothy Hackworth Museum (Shildon, Durham): Hackworth's house, works shed, displays – soon to be linked to new National Railway Museum outstation at Shildon: expected large engine and rolling stock in new great shed. National Railway Museum (Leeman Road, York):

NRM's second **Rocket** *replica is shown as a cutaway.*

greatest railway museum in the world, passenger-carrying replica of *Rocket*, replica of Trevithick Penydarren engine made to Gateshead design, NER and LNER exhibits, electric Quayside locomotive, statue of George Stephenson, comprehensive displays. Science Museum (Exhibition Road, London): original *Rocket* (1829), *Puffing Billy* (1814), displays. Royal Museum of Scotland (Chambers Street, Edinburgh): *Wylam Dilly* (1814) decorates the café.

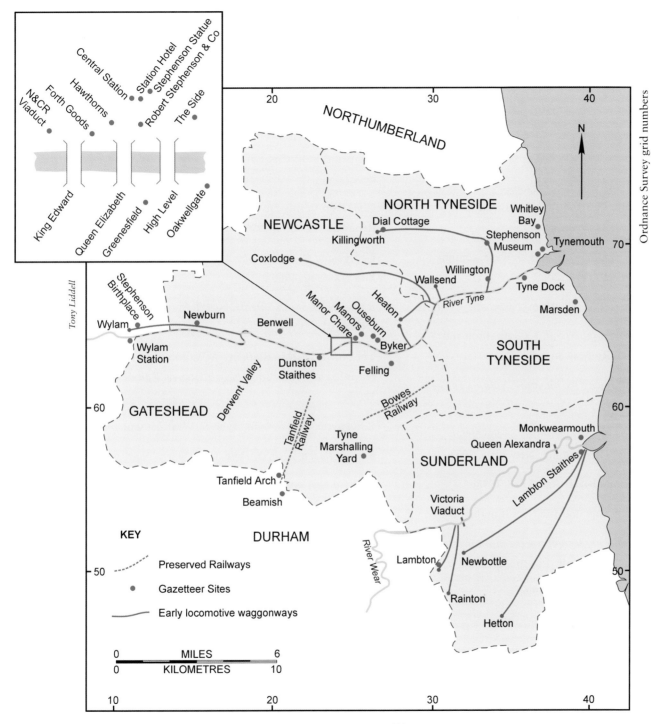

Inset (top left):
N&CR Viaduct · Forth Goods · Hawthorns · Central Station · Station Hotel · Stephenson Statue · Stephenson & Co · Robert Stephenson & Co · The Side
King Edward · Queen Elizabeth · Greenesfield · High Level · Oakwellgate

Ordnance Survey grid numbers

N

NORTHUMBERLAND

NORTH TYNESIDE

Whitley Bay
Stephenson Museum
Tynemouth

70

NEWCASTLE

Dial Cottage
Killingworth

Coxlodge

Willington
Wallsend

Tyne Dock

Heaton
Ouseburn
Manors
Manor Chare
Byker

River Tyne

Marsden

SOUTH TYNESIDE

Tony Liddell

Stephenson Birthplace
Wylam
Newburn
Benwell

Wylam Station
Dunston Staithes
Felling

Denwent Valley

Bowes Railway

60

GATESHEAD

Tanfield Railway

Tyne Marshalling Yard

SUNDERLAND

60

Monkwearmouth
Queen Alexandra

Lambton Staithes

Tanfield Arch

Beamish

Victoria Viaduct

DURHAM

50

KEY

Lambton
Newbottle

- - - - Preserved Railways

Rainton

River Wear

● Gazetteer Sites

Hetton

50

—— Early locomotive waggonways

MILES
0 — — — 6
KILOMETRES
0 — — — 10

10 · 20 · 30 · 40

For an area of this small size, the concentration of sites of international, as well as of national importance in railway history, is unmatched anywhere in the world.

153

FURTHER READING

The Great Metro Guide to Tyne & Wear, Vernon Abbott and Roy Chapman (Hawes, 1990).

The High Level Bridge and Newcastle Central Station, John Addyman and Bill Fawcett (Newcastle, 1999).

The archaeological excavation of wooden waggonway remains at Lambton D Pit, Sunderland, Ian Ayris et al. In *Industrial Archaeology Review*, Volume XX, 1998.

A Guide to the Industrial Archaeology of Tyne & Wear, compiled Ian Ayris and Stafford M. Linsley (1994).

The First Locomotive Engineers, L.G. Charlton (Newcastle, 1974).

Industrial Locomotives of Northumberland, L.G. Charlton and Colin E. Mountford (Industrial Railway Society, 1983).

A History of North Eastern Railway Architecture: Volume 1: The Pioneers, Bill Fawcett (2001).

The Art of Mining: Thomas Hair's Watercolours of the Great Northern Coalfield, by Douglas Glendinning (Newcastle, 2000).

Newcastle's Railways, Ken Groundwater (Ian Allen, 1998).

Early Railways, edited by Andy Guy and Jim Rees (London, 2001).

Coals on Rails, or the reason for my wrighting: the autobiography of Anthony Errington, ed. by P.E.H. Hair (Liverpool, 1988).

Rail Centre: Newcastle, K. Hoole (London, 1986).

Early Wooden Railways, M.J.T. Lewis (London, 1970).

Crossing the Tyne, Frank Manders and Richard Potts (Newcastle, 2001).

The Bowes Railway, Colin Mountford (Industrial Railway Society, 1966).

Industrial Locomotives of Durham, Colin E. Mountford and L.G. Charlton (Industrial Railway Society, 1977). A new edition is imminent.

Civil Engineering Heritage: Northern England, edited by R.W. Rennison (London, 1996).

George and Robert Stephenson: the Railway Revolution, L.T.C. Rolt (London, 1960).

Railways of South Shields, Neil T. Sinclair & Ian S. Carr (Newcastle, 1990).

The North Eastern Railway, W.W. Tomlinson (Newcastle [1915], reprinted as *Tomlinson's North Eastern Railway*, Newton Abbot, 1967).

Railways of Sunderland, Tyne & Wear Museums Service (1986).

Rails between Wear & Tyne, C.R. Warn (Newcastle, n.d.).

Waggonways and early railways of Northumberland, C.R. Warn (1976).

The Railways of Northumberland and Newcastle upon Tyne 1828-1998, J.A. Wells (Newcastle, 1998).

Suburban Railways of Tyneside, Alan Young (Leeds, 1999).

Index to major names and places